Another Introduction to Programming with Java Book

Another Introduction to Programming with Java Book

Copyright © 2016 By Tim Talbot

Contents

This page intentionally blank

Chapter 1: Introduction
About Me and Why I Decided To Write This Book

I was a 90's kid. I grew up in the era of dial-up and online text based games. It was around this time that I first took an interest in how a computer program does what it does. My first exposure to any form of programming was a scripting language within an IRC client and it was horrendous to say the least. Fascinated by what it could achieve, I moved on to something I considered to be much more useful - HTML. I wanted to make the text based games I was playing at the time. Shortly following my initial studies of HTML, I ventured deeper into the workings of the internet and deciphered tools and concepts unknown and new to me such as web servers, databases and server side scripting. My point is, as a child trying to learn these technologies I never really managed to grasp anything the first time round and always felt that they could be explained much more clearly; for example, it took me several attempts with plenty of time off in between to fully comprehend just how to go about running a local web server. Port forwarding was a nightmare! Perhaps this is the reason many non-fiction authors put pen to paper nowadays, I guess!

Following my web development ventures, I moved on to C++ and found console (command line) applications quite interesting, especially once I moved past the simple stuff and started touching on object oriented programming (OOP). I decided to start learning Java the first time round when I hit pointers in C++ as they were such a horrid concept to wrap my head around at the time. Java was easy enough to pick up as the syntax is not unlike the syntax of C++. Of course, there was some Visual Basic thrown in there somewhere but I like to pretend I've never heard of it! Pretty much all programming related work at university was based on Java.

This has resulted in upwards of 12 years of self study followed by 3 years of professional education and over that length of time I have gained a great understanding of Java and programming in general. So, in essence, the reason I decided to write this book was to hopefully provide you with a much more concise, organised and clear way of learning the basics of programming with Java in a way that I wish was available to me at the time I began learning the language. My intentions were to convey the core concepts of Java as best I can with as little content as possible, getting straight to the point without too much crap in between, in order to make the book a quick read without missing anything important. A difficult compromise to reach and I hope I've done it right for you guys!

Who this book is for

This book is for anyone wanting to learn Java. Whether you're a beginner and have no knowledge of programming whatsoever, or you're an intermediate Java programmer and want to better understand some of the more advanced topics in this book, this book is for you. It's written with the beginner in mind but segmented in a way that means that the example code and exercises don't make you go searching through previous chapters to understand what's going on, unless you need to know what's going on!

Conventions used in this book

When referring to names of classes, variables, methods or keywords I will use *italic* font unless I forget; I'm only human!

Exercises

If you see this heading then there are some simple exercises for you to do relating to the information you've just read. Of course, nobody is forcing you to do them (unless you have a Jedi next to you working some mind tricks, but this isn't ideal) but they are intended to help you further understand the information they are being applied to. Solutions to these exercises can be found at the back of the book if answers are needed. I know, it's a pain in the ass and always drives me crazy too but what's the point in having a challenge if the answer is on the same page?! I will aim to include these exercises at the end of every key topic and, naturally, they will gradually increase in time consumption and difficulty.

Key Points

If you see this heading then you should take a few moments to study the points following it and make sure you understand them clearly. Similarly to the exercises, these will gradually increase in complexity but I will explain them in each section as clearly as possible.

There will be many times I just spam you with pages of code. Don't be disheartened, copy it out and compile it (I check every piece of source code before introducing it to the book to ensure it works so if it doesn't and you're sure you've got it right, email me!) and seek to understand it. The methodology is to give you the code and then explain it once you've written it out and tried it for yourself. That way, you will have at least a partial understanding of it before I dissect it piece by piece. Sometimes I may do it backwards, depending on what topics I'm discussing.

Finally, you will notice a lot of tables in the beginning of this book - this is because tables are the most effective and clear way of presenting information that can be found easily and referred back to when needed.

Problems with this book

At the end of this book lies an email address, this can be used to report any errors, typos or other problems with this book if you stumble across such problems. If there are indeed errors, they will be put on my website at:

http://timtalbot.co.uk/aitpwjb/

aitpwjb = Another Introduction to Programming with Java Book, in case you're curious like me.

The purpose of this is to ensure that you're not running into problems whilst reading through the book, because I've read books with errors in the past and let's face it, they suck!

Chapter 2: Where to Begin

Quick Overview

I'm sure that you all know what Java is and the applications of it, but if not - here's a quick overview. Java is a programming language that first came to light in 1995. It takes much of its syntax from C and C++ and was created with the specific intention of eradicating as many implementation dependencies as possible. It is an object oriented language and is completely platform independent. This is because, unlike, say, a native C++ program compiled on the platform it is intended for where the compiler translates source code directly into machine code, when Java is compiled the source is converted into class files containing byte code which is then *interpreted* by the Java Virtual Machine (JVM) on whatever platform the class file is run on. The drawbacks here, of course, are that interpreted programs run a little slower (although this is virtually unnoticeable with modern processing power) than native programs and the requirement of the Java Runtime Environment (JRE) to be installed on a target computer.

Due to the flexibility of the JVM, Java is used anywhere from mobile phones and web applications to ATMs, banks and televisions. Java is quite a popular choice when developing client-server applications such as high throughput chat systems.

How to write a Java program

Primarily, there are 2 ways you can go about writing a Java program and compiling it. You could use a simple text editor and compile it via the terminal / console / command line or you could use an Integrated Development Environment such as Eclipse or NetBeans. An IDE is simple enough to install so I haven't detailed the process in this book but you can find Eclipse at www.eclipse.org which is what I recommend, simply because it's what I use and maybe I am a little biased. I generally stick to a simple text editor when writing short programs and an IDE when working on larger projects and for this reason, throughout this book I have just used Windows Notepad. Java source files have a .java file extension.

Setting up the Development Environment

As previously mentioned, I'll be working on Windows and this means I will be using the command line to compile and run my Java code. The first thing needed is the Java Development Kit (JDK) which you can get from here:

http://www.oracle.com/technetwork/java/javase/downloads/

by going to this URL and clicking the download image link then selecting the appropriate version. Once installed, we will add the JDK *bin* directory to the System Environment Variables variable "Path". If you know how to do this, go ahead! If not, follow these instructions:

You have to right-click on the 'My Computer' (or 'This PC' as it says these days) icon on your desktop or start menu and select "properties":

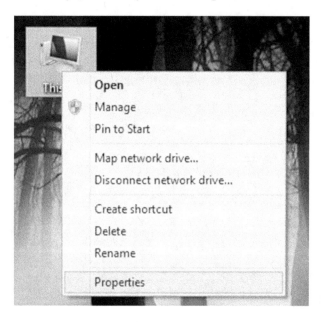

This will open the System screen which you then have to click "Advanced system settings" located in the left side panel:

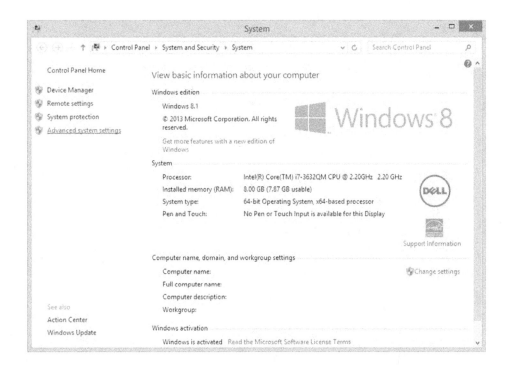

Advanced System settings looks like this:

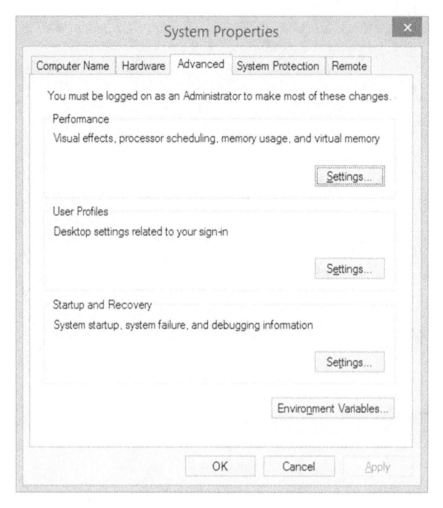

Finally, click "Environment Variables..." to get to the place we need to be.

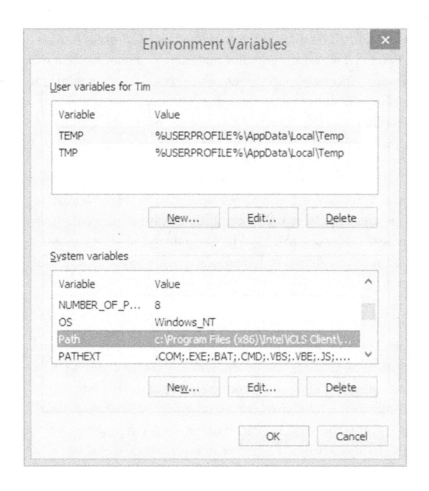

Once at the "Environment Variables" screen, scroll down under the "System variables" section until you see "Path", select it then click "Edit...". The last thing on the string in the edit box needs to be a semi-colon so if it isn't, put one in there. Then we are going to add the absolute file path to the JDK *bin* directory which should look something like this:

C:\Program Files\Java\jdk<version>\bin

Where *jdk<version>* is replaced with your Java version number such as *jdk1.8.0_45* for example. We've just gone through all this effort to save us the trouble of having to type that path every time we want to compile and/or run a Java program via the command line. To test that we've done it correctly, launch cmd (hold the windows key and press R, type "cmd" and hit enter) then type "java" and hit enter. You should see a wall of text appear that lists the usage options of the java.exe executable; you *don't* want to see "'java' is not recognized as an internal or external command, operable program or batch file". If you do, go through these steps again slowly and make sure you haven't overlooked anything.

You can now close all of the dialogs we have opened. Next, we are going to create a "Java" directory, anywhere you like, which will contain all of our source code and class files. It'll be our little box for working in. Just don't forget where it is as we will have to navigate to this directory via the command line. Now all this is done, we are ready to move on to our first simple program.

Using Command Line (Windows Only)

This book makes the assumption that you know how to open command-line and navigate it but in case you don't, here's a brief look at that. If you're running Linux then you're on your own because, let's face it, Linux is not a place for n00bs! If you're running Mac, you're going to want to open Terminal and use *ls* instead of *dir*. As for setting up environment variables described in the previous section, that'll be something for non-Windows users to figure out for themselves =)

So, opening the Command Line on Windows - Hold the Windows key and hit R, this'll open the "Run..." window in which you're going to type "cmd" and hit enter, thus the command line window is opened!

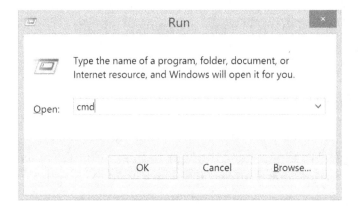

Use the command *dir* to list the contents of your current directory and use *cd* to change directory. You can type the full path of your *Java* directory like so:

cd C:\some_path\some_directory

Now you're ready to continue.

Hello, World! (Compiling your first program)

So, Hello, World! You may be familiar with this if you have done any programming in the past. It's probably the most iconic and notable programming introduction there is. It simply consists of a short program that prints out the text "Hello, World!" and contributes to the satisfaction of writing your first program. So here it is:

```
class HelloWorld { //start of class

    public static void main(String[] args) {

        System.out.println("Hello, World!");

    }

} //end of class
```

That's it! If you take this code and place it inside a text file named "HelloWorld.java" within your *Java* directory, paying close attention to the capitalization and spacing (lack of) of the filename, you will be almost ready to compile and run your program. Be sure to change the "Save as type" to "All Files (*.*)" if using Windows to ensure your file is in fact a .java file. First, though, you must have the command line open and navigate to your *Java* directory. Once there you will type *javac HelloWorld.java* to compile your .java file. Once you have typed the command to compile your Java program, it is ready to run. To run it you must type *java HelloWorld*. The screenshot below shows this process and if all is well, there should be no errors and you will see "Hello, World!" printed into the command line console:

```
C:\Windows\system32\cmd.exe

d:\Desktop\java>javac HelloWorld.java

d:\Desktop\java>java HelloWorld
Hello, World!

d:\Desktop\java>
```

Notice the slight difference in command. The run command is "java" and the compile command is "javaC"

```
class HelloWorld
```

This first line is defining a class. The word *class* is a keyword in Java and is followed by the name of the class, beginning with a capital letter as is convention.

```
{ //start of class
```

The next line is simply the start of the class. Think of this curly brace as an open gate that has to be closed at a later stage. Opening braces always need matching closing braces. This line also shows a single line comment. Comments are included to remind you what particular code does or to help other programmers to understand your code; the compiler ignores comments.

```
public static void main(String[] args)
```

This is the declaration of the *main* method within your HelloWorld class. The *main* method is the main entry point of any program and is required for a Java class to be able to execute. The signature above (the way the method is defined) is how the *main* method should be defined and is how Java identifies the method as your program's entry point. The first two keywords *public* and *static* are referred to as modifiers and can be written in this order or swapped around, they will still work the same. The next word is *void* and, although this sounds sinister, it's simply a return type - methods *can* return data but the *main* method does not and thus it has a return type of nothing or *void*. Next is the word *main*. This is the name of our method. You can create a *main()* method perfectly legally without any arguments that is not a program's entry point but I would consider this bad practice simply because of the potential confusion. The *String[ ] args* is a *parameter* or *argument* of type *String[ ]*. It does not require the name *args* but *args* or *argv* are the conventional names of choice for this particular argument. Finally, the *[ ]* of *String[ ]* denotes that the argument is an array and can contain more than one value. This explanation may come across as quite a mountain of information at first, for one little line, but will make much more sense once we look at variables and methods so try not to get too caught up on it for now!

```
    {

        System.out.println("Hello, World!");

    }

} //end of class
```

The next three lines are easily explained. The first and third line, the opening and closing braces, are opening and closing the *main* method and all code between these belongs to the *main* method. This is referred to as the body of a method. The line in between, *System.out.println("Hello, World!");* is simply printing the text we want to display. This is called a statement and all statements end with a semi-colon. This line could be explained in a lot more detail but that goes far beyond this scope of this tutorial. Finally, the closing brace of the class follows the closing brace of the *main* method along with another demonstration of a comment.

Just one more fairly important conventional effect here is the indentation. Notice that after every opening brace the indentation increases by 1 tab press (or 4 spaces, depending on how you like to indent) and decreases by 1 tab press after every closing brace. This is important for the sake of readability. It's so much more difficult to find a missing closing brace without proper indentation and believe me, it's quite common to miss a closing brace here and there from time to time!

Hello World is boring!

We've done Hello, World! and it's an incredibly simplistic program to say the least. It takes a little time to understand if you are new to programming but even so, you might be looking for something a little bit more advanced just to get stuck in. So here it is, I'm throwing you in at the deep end right now!

```java
//import class needed to read from console
import java.util.Scanner;

class HelloWorldIsBoring {

    //declare variable to read from console
    static Scanner in = new Scanner(System.in);

    public static void main(String[] args) {

        //ask user what to do
        System.out.println("What shall I do for
                        you?");
        System.out.println("1)Repeat your name\n
                        2)Repeat your age\n
            3)Run away and hide (exit program)");

        //variable declaration and assignment
        int response=0;
        //(advanced) error catching
        try {
            //get user response
            response =
                Integer.parseInt(in.nextLine());
        }
        catch(NumberFormatException nfe) {
        //if response is not a number...
            //tell user of error and die
            System.out.println("You did not enter a
                number. Exiting program");
            //System.out.println(nfe.toString());

            System.exit(0);
        }

        //declare string variable
        String temp=""; //store response

        //flow control switch statement
        switch(response) {
            case 1:
                System.out.print("What is your
                name? ");
```

```java
                temp = in.nextLine();
                System.out.println("Hello, " +
                                        temp);
            break;

            case 2:

                System.out.println("How old are
                                    you?");
                temp = in.nextLine();
                System.out.println("You are " +
                                temp + " years old!");
            break;

            case 3:
                System.out.println("Exiting
                                        program!");
                System.exit(0);
            break;

            default:
                System.out.println("Unknown
                    Command. Exiting Program!");
                System.exit(0);
            break;
        }//end switch
    }//end main()
}//end class
```

Key Points

1) All Java programs must contain a main entry point to be executed; the main() method
2) All Java programs must start with a class definition
3) All opening braces must have matching closing braces
4) Indent your code
5) Comment your code

Exercises

1) Convert your original Hello World program into the one above if you haven't already
2) What does \n do?
3) Change the name of the *Scanner* variable throughout the code, recompile and run it to familiarize yourself with renaming variables.
4) What is the signature for the main method in order for it to be recognised as the main entry point of a program by Java
5) Don't get too caught up on any stuff you don't understand here, all will be explained in the coming chapters

Formatting

Just a quick mention on the code formatting used within this book because, as you can imagine, trying to get a long line of code on to a page like this isn't the easiest of tasks. I will be using the same formatting throughout for each bit of code and the format is as follows:

```
methodOrClass() {
    //one tab
    ifOrSwitch() {
        //two tabs
    }
}
```

If a method or statement is too long to fit on one line, it **will** be on one line within the source code, just not within the book. Every continuous line will be tabbed as far as possible to make code snippets more readable. So if we have a method called *someMethod()* which takes 5 arguments, it's going to go onto another line and will be written like so:

```
void someMethod(int arg1, int arg2, int arg3, int arg4,
                                               int arg5) {
```

Chapter 3: Variables and Operators
What is a variable?

Variables hold data. Different types of variable hold different types of data. I like to think of a variable as a toddler's shape sorter; only the right shapes can fit into the right slots. It's name comes from the fact that **usually**, the value of a variable can vary/change. They are used to store data in programs. We have already seen variable declarations in the last chapter so now we will look at them in more detail including primitive types and scope (from where your variables can be seen within your program). Variables may also be referred to as member variables or fields. A variable name may contain numbers but should not start with them; underscores and the dollar sign can also be used within a variable name and **can** be used at the start of the variable name, however the dollar sign is never used and the underscore seldom appears at the beginning of a variable, owing to convention. Finally, the typical convention for naming variables is non-cryptic names that start with a lower case word and each following word is capitalized, also known as camel-case. See the examples below depicting how one would expect to see naming conventions used on a variable name, each separated by a comma.

```
variableOne, variable1, VARIABLE_ONE, sensibleVariableName
//acceptable

1var //illegal

v1, vOne //ok but cryptic

_variable1 //ok but against convention

VariableOne, Variable //ok but against convention (note
the upper case V)
```

Also, words defined as keywords in Java cannot be used as variable names, Java keywords are listed at https://wikipedia.org/wiki/List_of_Java_keywords if you want to take a look over them but the compiler will always let you know if you try to use a keyword as a variable name, although it might not always be clear.

First of all, here's a standard chart depicting primitive data types, examples of data stored within them and their limits in Java - there are 8 in total:

Type	Examples	Limits	Explanation
int (integer)	1, 3, 5, 204, -19892	-2^{31} to 2^{31}-1	A 32 bit signed integer
byte	-128, 127	-128-127	8 bit signed integer
short	328, -232, 2,32	-32768-32767	16 bit signed integer
long	832, 3115,4851,-13515,-134	-2^{63} - 2^{63} OR, in Java SE 8 and above, 0 - 2^{64}-1	a 64 bit signed integer but can also be used as a 64 bit unsigned integer in Java SE 8 and later
float	0.0102030f, 9.2384F	The limits of float and double exceed the scope of this chapter	single-precision 32 bit floating point number
double	3832.283828, 31.28383d	The limits of float and double exceed the scope of this chapter	double-precision 64 bit floating point number
boolean	true, false	true, false	Represents a true/false condition
char (character)	a, b, c, d, 1, e, k, m, z, 0	\u0000 - \uffff 0-65535	single 16 bit unicode character

Generally speaking, you'll use *int* for integer type values - whole numbers, *double* for decimal numbers, *char* for single characters and *boolean* as a flag to determine a true/false condition. Unless you're writing a program that will be flooded with data and thus you begin to care about memory usage, you won't really need to worry about *byte* or *short*. *long*, on the other hand, is very useful if you need numbers larger than (or smaller than, negatives) those supported by the *int* data type. When deciding whether to use *float* or *double*, the main things to consider are how precise you need your stored data to be and whether or not you need to be conservative with memory. When representing decimal numbers, *double* is generally the data type of choice as it can hold more precise values. Neither *float* nor *double* should be used for precise values such as currency in programs written for purposes other than learning. The BigDecimal class in the java.math package should be used instead but this goes far beyond the scope of this chapter. Following is a demonstration of how each of these primitive data types are declared and initialized. To declare a variable is to create it and to initialize a variable is to give it some data.

```
int a; // simple uninitialized declaration of an integer
       // called 'a'

int a = 0; // simple declaration of an integer called 'a'
           // and initialized with a value of zero

char c = '\0'; // char declaration called 'c' and
               // initialization of zero

               // note the single quotations that a
               // required to provide a value to a char
               // variable

boolean f = true; // boolean value set to true
```

Integer literals can be defined directly in code in decimal, hexadecimal and binary. To define a hexadecimal number you must prefix your hexadecimal representation with 0x and similarly with binary definitions, you must prefix your binary number with 0b. An integer is of type *long* if it is suffixed with an L, otherwise it is of type *int*.

Floating point literals become a bit strange. A literal of type *float* should end with F or f; if not, its type is *double* but *double*'s do not have to end with D or d **but** they optionally can. I tend to use **d** at the end of all *double* values in order to ensure Java treats them as *double*. Scientific notation can be used when defining the value of a *double* by using E or e. The following two values are the same and demonstrate this scientific notation:

```
double a = 5000.0;

double b = 5e3;
```

Finally, another cool thing is that when defining numeric literals, you can use an underscore within them to aid readability. This applies to Java SE 7 and above. There are of course limitations to this and they are as such:

- You cannot place an underscore at the beginning or end of a number,
- Next to a decimal point in a floating point literal,
- Prior to an F, L or D suffix
- or where a string of digits is expected

for example:

```
long ccnum = 1111_2222_3333_4444L;
```

is the same as this:

```
long ccnum = 1111222233334444L;
```

Strings

A *String* (note the capital S) is a string of *char* characters and is not technically considered as a primitive data type although it is generally thought of as one due to the support given to it by Java. Factually, though, the *String* is a simple data object. Strings can be used to store words, sentences, telephone numbers or any other string of characters. This is done in the same way as declaring any other variable.

```
String s = "Hello, World!";
```

Type Casting

Type casting or just casting is the process of converting one variable to another, casting one variable type to another. For example, if we have a floating-point number of 250.0F but we want it to be an integer, we can force it to become an integer with casting. The general syntax of casting is:

```
oldType var1 = some_value;

newType var2 = (newType) var1;
```

Here, the variable *var1* of type *oldType* is casted to the *newType* type in order to assign the value to the *newType* variable *var2*. This is much more easily demonstrated in code with the example I mentioned above:

```
float var1 = 250.0F;

int var2 = (int) var1;
```

Give this a try and see what happens when you cast a floating-point value to an integer when the value after the decimal is not 0.

```
class castExample {

    public static void main(String[] args) {

        float var1 = 250.152F;

        int var2 = (int) var1;

        System.out.println("var 1 = " + var1);

        System.out.println("var 2 = " + var2);

    }

} //end class
```

Arrays

An array is simply a collection of variables under the same name with a unique index to select an *element* from the array of data. Any of the data types we have talked about so far can be used in an array. To declare an array, we use the following syntax:

```
int[] a = new int[10];
```

Where *new* indicates that we are allocating enough memory for 10 integer variables. To access these elements within our new *a* array, we must use a unique index which starts from zero and goes up to the number of elements minus 1, in this case this number is 10-1=9. This is both how we would access and assign values to the elements of our *a* array:

```
a[0] = 4;

a[1] = 2;

a[2] = 3;

a[3] = 8;

a[4] = 7;

a[5] = 5;

a[6] = 4;

a[7] = 9;

a[8] = 7;

a[9] = 1;
```

For each of the 10 elements in our *a* array, we have assigned an integer value. This is essentially a collection of data and is better represented by an image.

4	2	3	8	7	5	4	9	7	1
0	1	2	3	4	5	6	7	8	9

The numbers in the top row are the array values and the numbers in the bottom row are the indices (index, plural) for a 10 element integer array.

We can also declare and initialize an array in the same statement like so:

```
int[] a = {4, 2, 3, 8, 7, 5, 4, 9, 7, 1};
```

This shorthand version will create an integer array with *x* elements where *x* is the number of values found between the curly braces and separated by commas. This example will create the same 10 element *int* array we created in our first example above.

There is also such a thing as multidimensional arrays which are useful for representing grids or matrices but I will not be covering those here. For more information regarding multidimensional arrays, please visit the Java documentation online.

The *final* keyword

All variables are subject to change either intentionally or otherwise but you may want to avoid this. For example, if you're working on a collaborative project and add a new variable that shouldn't be changed or you just want to avoid accidentally changing a variable within your own projects, the *final* keyword comes in handy. To achieve this, variables can be prefixed with the keyword *final*. This is also referred to as a *constant* variable and means that once the variable is initialized (assigned a value) it cannot be changed and if you try to do so, you will get a compiler error. This keyword can also be used in relation to classes and methods.

Variable Scope

The term 'scope' in programming is used to describe where, within code, a variable is visible, the accessibility of the variable throughout the program. Firstly, a variable can be declared one of 4 places:

1. within the class body
2. as a method argument
3. within the body of a method
4. within a code block such as an *if-statement* or *while loop*

If a variable is declared within the class body, it is accessible from any point within the class, including within the body of a method or a code block. This is referred to as a global variable or global scope. A variable declared as a method argument/parameter is only accessible to that method, the same is true of variables declared within the body of a method or a code block. These are called local variables. If a variable is declared within the class body and then another variable with the same name is declared within a method, for example, the local variable takes the lead role within the method. In order to access the variable declared within the class body, the 'this' keyword is used.

A variable cannot be accessed *before* it is declared.

```
class FeelTheVars
{

    static int globalVariable = 0;

    public static void main(String[] args)
    {
        int localVariableOne = 1;

        int localVariableTwo = 2;

        System.out.println("globalVariable: " +
                        globalVariable);

        System.out.println("localVariableOne: " +
                        localVariableOne);

        System.out.println("localVariableTwo: " +
                        localVariableTwo);

        methodWithVariable(3);
    }

    private static void methodWithVariable(int
                                        argumentVariable)
    {
        int localVariableInMethod=4;

        System.out.println("globalVariable: " +
                        globalVariable);

        System.out.println("argumentVariable: " +
                        argumentVariable);

        System.out.println("localVariableInMethod: " +
                        localVariableInMethod);
    }
}
```

The above code is intended to depict the usage of variables in different locations. Do copy it out, it's a boring but essential stage in learning how to program! Don't worry about the 'static' keyword used here, remove it and see what happens when you try to compile the code.

Operators

An operator is simply a special symbol that performs a function on one, two or three operands. The most common operator is the *assignment* operator and is used every time you assign a value to a variable; this operator is the equals (=) sign:

```
int x = 10;
```

This operator assigns a value on the right of the expression, 10, to the *operand* on the left, *x*.

Arithmetic Operators

Symbol	Example	Purpose

+	y = y+10;
	or
	y += 10;
		Addition operator; also used for string concatenation

-	y = y-10;
	or
	y -= 10;
		Subtraction operator

/	y = y/10;
	or
	y /= 10;
		Division operator

*	y = y*10;
	or
	y *= 10;
		Multiplication Operator

%	y = y%10;
	or
	y %= 10;
		The remainder operator which gives the remainder of a division sum; also known as the mod or modulo operator

Arithmetic expressions that are combined with the assignment operator to look like this:

```
y += 10;
```

They are called compound assignments.

The arithmetic plus (+) can also be used to concatenate (link together, join) two or more strings to form a single string, like so:

```
String x = "hello";

String y = "world";

String z = x + " " + y; //space between the strings
```

or

```
z = x + y; //no space between the strings
```

Symbol	Example	Purpose
+	+5, +101, +28419	indicates a positive value (omitted by default as numbers are positive without this symbol)
-	-1,-135,-31,-2	indicates a negative value; negates an expression

++	`int x = 10;`
	`x++;`
	`++x;`
		Increment operator. Increases a value by 1

--	`int x = 30;`
	`x--;`
	`--x;`
		the decrement operator. Decreases a value by 1

!	`boolean f = true;` `f = !f;`	This is known as the logical complement operator according to Java documentation *but* is generally referred to as the *not* operator. This will invert the value of a boolean.

The next two tables below (Comparison and Conditional) are based on the following variables for the purpose of demonstration:

```
int x=10, y=20, z=10; //yes, you can declare variables
like this in Java
```

These operators are all used for the comparison of one value vs another and as such the result will return a boolean value of true or false.

Symbol	Example	Purpose
==	x == 10 returns true	To determine whether two values are equal (equal to)
!=	x != 10 returns false	to determine whether two values are *not* equal (not equal to)
>	x > z returns false	To determine whether the left value is greater than the right value (greater than)
>=	x >= z returns true	To determine whether the left value is greater than **or** equal to the right value (greater than **or** equal to)
<	x < 20 returns true	To determine whether the left value is less than the right value (less than)
<=	15 <= y returns true	To determine whether the left value is less than **or** equal to the right value (less than **or** equal to)

Symbol	Example	Purpose
&&	`x == 10 && x != y returns true`	The conditional AND operator where both parts of the conditional statement have to be satisfied in order for the statement to be true
||	`x == 15 || x == y`	The conditional OR operator where only one of two parts of the conditional statement have to be satisfied in order for the statement to be true
?:	`x == 10 ? true : false`	The ternary operator which is effectively shorthand for if-then-else (if condition is met, true, else false) but you will most likely understand this better after we look at the Conditional Statements chapter

The *conditional AND* operator takes precedence over the *conditional OR* operator and as such it is evaluated first in the event that you decide to use both operators within the same expression. Both of these operators function on a short-circuit basis (according to Java documentation) and this means that they will only evaluate as much as necessary so if the left hand expression is false, the right hand expression will not be evaluated if the conditional AND operator has been used, for example.

Key Points

1. *Variables* are also called *fields, members* or *member variables*
2. You must select the correct data type for the data you will store in your variable
3. The plus sign (+) is also used for joining strings together (String concatenation)
4. Strings are not technically primitive data types but are generally thought as such due to the support given to them by Java

Chapter 4: Access Modifiers

Access modifiers are keywords used to control access to a particular field (variable) or method of a class or the class itself. These keywords are *public, private* and *protected*. Classes are said to be controlled by *top level access control* and member fields and methods by *member level access control*.

Top Level Access Control:

This is intended to control access to classes and can either be *public* or *package-private* (which has no specific modifier keyword). A class declared with the *public* modifier is visible to all classes within a project, regardless of package, and if no modifier is used, *package-private*, the class is only visible to classes within the same package.

Examples of this in use are as follows:

```
public TestClass {
```

or, simply,

```
TestClass {
```

Member Level Access Control:

Member level access control refers to controlling the access to methods and fields within a class. Firstly, you can use the *public* keyword or omit a keyword in the same way, and with the same meanings, as above. Further to this, you can use the *protected* or *private* modifiers. The *private* modifier allows access only from within the same class and the *protected* modifier gives access to methods and fields from within the same package, similarly to *package-private*, but with the addition of allowing access via a subclass of the class in another package. Following is a table illustrating the levels of access, similar to that found within the Java documentation:

Modifier	Class	Package	Subclass	World
public	Yes	Yes	Yes	Yes
protected	Yes	Yes	Yes	No
modifier not used	Yes	Yes	No	No
private	Yes	No	No	No

The first column indicates which modifier is being referenced. This is followed by whether or not the modifier provides access to the class it is used in (the class column) and then the package the class is contained in (the package column). Then if the modifier allows access within a subclass of the class it is used in (the subclass column) and finally whether the modifier allows access from **any** class within any package (the world column).

One of the key purposes of access modifiers is to ensure errors from misuse of your class cannot happen if your class is used by other programmers. When deciding which access modifiers to use, you should always go with *private* unless you have a reason not to and avoid *public* fields except for *constants* or unless you have a reason to do so.

Key Points

1. Always use *private* unless you have a reason not to
2. Only use *public* for constants unless you have a reason to use it elsewhere
3. Understand the difference between the access modifiers
4. Access Modifiers exist to reduce errors when other programmers use your code

Chapter 5: Conditional statements, Flow Control

What are conditionals?

At some point in your program you will want to make a decision and act on it accordingly. Conditionals let you do this - you can ask a question, so to speak, and do one thing or another depending on whether the answer is yes or no. You will probably need to use conditionals almost all the time so understanding them is of some importance. Firstly, conditionals may also simply be referred to as *if-statements* or *if-else statements* and this is because of the keywords *if* and *else* that you will use when writing your conditional statements. Here is where we use the relational and equality operators and the conditional operators from the chapter 3.

If statements

The straight forward *if* looks like this:

```
if (true) {

    //do something

}
```

This says *if true is true* then execute the code within the code block (within the curly braces). Of course, this example will always be true as there is not a conditional statement as such.

Here is a practical example:

```
if (age >= 18) {

  System.out.println("User is old enough to buy alcohol in the UK");

}
```

So, if the variable called *age* has a value that is greater than or equal to the number 18 then the output of the program will be "*User is old enough to buy alcohol in the UK*". If the condition is not met, nothing will happen.

So in a nutshell, that's the simple use of an *if-statement*. The *expression* is the conditional statement that comes between the opening and closing bracket of the *if*. More complex statements can also be written, see below:

```
if(age >=18 && age < 70) {

    System.out.println("The user is between 18 and 69
                        years of age");

}

if(age >=18 && age < 70 && dob_month != 12) {

    System.out.println("The user is between 18 and 69
            years of age and was not born in December");

}

if(age >=18 || dob_month != 12) {

    System.out.println("The user is 18 or over or was not
                        born in December");

}
```

These three examples here demonstrate the use of the *conditional AND* and *conditional OR* operators.

The first of the three says that *if the variable 'age' has a value that is greater than or equal to 18 AND the variable 'age' has a value that is less than 70 then execute the code within the if block.* The expression is only true if both of the conditions are met.

The second *if* extends the first and adds an extra condition to check whether the user's month of birth is December or not; the expression is false if either condition is not met. This expression says *if the variable 'age' has a value that is greater than or equal to 18 AND the variable 'age' has a value that is less than 70 AND the variable 'dob_month' has a value that does NOT equal 12 then execute the code within the if block.*

Finally, the third example uses the *conditional OR* operator within the expression. It can be read as follows: *if the variable 'age' has a value greater than or equal to 18 OR the variable 'dob_month' has a value not equal to 12 then execute the code within the if block.*

As you can see, this only provides us a way of executing code if our expression is true. If it is false, we may want to execute some alternative code and this is where the *else* clause of an *if statement* comes in.

else-if statements

else-if statements allow us to provide an additional conditional statement in what is essentially a chain of conditional statements. If our first *if-statement* condition is false the code can move on to an *else-if* statement. If the *else-if* statement is false, the code can move on to another *else-if* statement and you can have as many as you like. For example, see the code below:

```java
if(age >=18 && dob_month != 12) {

    System.out.println("The user is 18 or over and was not
                        born in December");

}

else if (dob_month == 12) {

    System.out.println("The user was born in December");

}
```

So here I have used the same if statement from the previous example, *if the variable 'age' has a value greater than or equal to 18 OR the variable 'dob_month' has a value not equal to 12 then execute the code within the if block,* but now we add to this ... *else if the variable 'dob_month' has a value equal to 12 then execute the code within the else-if block.*

This gives us a lot more flexibility with how to control the flow of our code and allows us to pose many more conditional statements should we need them.

else statements

else statements must follow an *if-statement* or an *else-if* statement, they cannot be used alone. They also have to be the last statement in a series of conditional statements, an *else-if* statement cannot follow an *else* statement, for example.

Essentially, an *else* statement says "if the *if-statement* is false, do this instead". See the examples below:

Valid

```
if(age >=18) {

    System.out.println("The user is 18 or over");

}

else if(age >= 10) {

        System.out.println("The user is between 10 and 17
                        years of age");

}

else {

    System.out.println("The user is under 10 years of
                        age");

}
```

<u>Valid</u>

```
if(age >=18) {

    System.out.println("The user is 18 or over");

}

else {

    System.out.println("The user is under 18 years of
                        age");

}
```

<u>Invalid</u>

```
else {

    System.out.println("The user is under 18 years of
                        age");

}
```

The Ternary Operator

The *ternary* operator is simply shorthand for *if-then-else* code. They can be nested; to have one ternary statement inside another and so on. The ternary operator is a personal favourite of mine simply because it looks cool and is generally written on one line of code. A good typical use of the ternary operator is to assign a variable a particular value based on a condition. Here are a couple of examples of this in action.

```
int x = 10;

int y = 15;

int z = (y==x) ? x+y : x;
```

```
z = (y==x) ? x : (y>x) ? y : x;
```

So let's break this code down. The first 2 lines simply create a couple of variables, x and y, and give them a value (declaration and initialization). The third line creates an integer too but this time, its value is determined by an *if-then-else* statement using the ternary (?:) operator. This is in the form of:

(condition) ? result if true: result if false

So, based on the values defined, the value of *z* becomes 10 because:

if (15==10) is true then the value of z is 10+15 otherwise the value of z is 10.

The final line of code here assigns a new value to *z*, again using the ternary operator but this time a nested condition is included. If the original condition is false, another condition is evaluated. Based on these evaluations, the new value of *z* becomes 15; the greater number out of *x* and *y*. In simple English, this statement can be read as follows:

if (15 == 10) is true then the value of z is 10 otherwise if 15 is greater than 10 then the value of z is 15 otherwise the value of z is 10.

Despite their apparent complexity, this method of coding conditions is quite elegant, in my opinion. There isn't any massive performance increases from using ternary operations as opposed to *if-then-else* statements. There is the added benefit of providing concise code. One particular scenario where the ternary operator is the only option is if you need to initialize a *constant* based on a condition. A *constant* is a variable whose value cannot change once initialized, as mentioned in chapter 3.

Switch Statements

Switch statements, as shown in the *Hello World is boring!* program in the second chapter, are another type of flow control. Not quite the same as the *if* and *if-else* statements but very extremely useful nonetheless.

A switch statement, instead of having a plan of action for *true* and *false* scenarios, has a number of possible courses of action. The chosen course depends on a switch, which is essentially a variable. The switch can use *byte, int, char, short and String* along with a few special classes that wrap primitive data types but we'll ignore that, it's beyond our scope. We'll be using *integers* in our switch statements because they're the easiest to work with.

So let's assume you want to print out a particular response depending on a user input. You could write a dozen *if* statements that cater for each scenario which would work fine. You should decide which to use based on the data you are evaluating. *if* statements can evaluate ranges and sets of conditions whereas *switch* can only evaluate one value. Here's how we'd go about that:

```
int switcher = 0;

switch(switcher) {

        case 1:

                //do stuff

        break;

        case 2:

                //do other stuff

        break;

        case 3:

                //do other other stuff

        break;
```

```
default:

    //do default stuff

break;

}
```

As you can see, each decision within the *switch* is called a *case*. The *switch* attempts to match the given value to any cases; the code will be executed within the *case* if there is a match. Any code between *case x:* and *break;* will be executed. the **break** keyword is super important here, without it, any cases that execute will **fall through** which means that every case after the matched case will execute sequentially until the end of the *switch* block. This can cause all kinds of headache! Finally, there is a *default:* case which will execute if there are no matches, it is not compulsory but absolutely recommended. The data your *switch* statements evaluate can come from anywhere. In this example we use a simple *integer* variable but this could be set to something different based on user input, *if* statements or even calculations. We'll see a good example of using a *switch* statement in chapter 8.

Chapter 6: Loops

Java provides several types of loop for us to use. This chapter will take a look at each type of loop and the problems and benefits of loops. The two primary types of loop you will find yourself using are the *for* loop and the *while* loop, each having a couple of variations.

While loops

while loops essentially say "while this condition is true, do the stuff below". Here is a pseudo example of a simple *while* loop:

```
while(condition) {

    //do some stuff

}
```

The *while* loop is best utilized to execute a block of code an unknown number of times. The condition can be any expression that evaluates to true, as shown in the previous chapter regarding *conditionals*. Unlike an *if statement,* however, an expression within a *while* loop **must** evaluate to true in order for the loop to run, there are no *else while* loops. The primary benefit of a *while* loop is that you can repeatedly execute the same piece of code based on a condition. This may sound rather basic but that's because it is. You'll see shortly that not all loops work in this way.

while loops may be disadvantageous for some situations where you require keeping track of the current iteration of the loop (i.e. how many times the loop has executed) and for any code that needs to execute at least once before checking whether or not it should repeat itself. That's not to say you cannot use them for such situations though, because you will find yourself requiring loops based on a true/false condition **and** keeping track of the current iteration of the loop. To do this, we create a counter variable **outside** the loop. Counters should generally start at zero because anything that requires an index in Java is zero based, think back to arrays!

Enough text abuse, here are a couple of *while* loops to demonstrate their usage in a variety of scenarios. First up is a simple arithmetic expression which will become false after the loop runs several times:

```
int age = 10;

while(age < 18) {

        //You cannot drink until you are 18, come back next
        //year.

        age += 1; //add a year to age. Could also be written
                  //as age++; or as age = age + 1;

}
```

So this loop will run a total of 8 times, until the value of *age* is no longer less than 18. Notice that the variable used within the condition of the *while* loop is manipulated within the body of the loop. **This is incredibly important**. If this didn't happen, the loop would never end and we'd be stuck with an infinite loop, more on this soon.

Next is a *while* loop with a counter, so you can keep track of the number of iterations the loop has ran.

```
int count = 0; //remember to use more appropriate,
               //descriptive names

               //unlike this!
int randomData[] =
{100,200,300,400,500,600,700,800,900,1000};

int endOfLoop = 10; //or you could use randomData.length
                    //to get the number of elements within
                    //the array

while(count < endOfLoop) {

      System.out.println(randomData[count]);

      //print data from array
```

```
        count++; //increment the count var

}

//don't forget that array indices start at 0
```

This loop has the benefit of a counter which allows us to access each element of the *randomData* array sequentially and print the values out to the user. We also use the counter as part of the condition to ensure the loop exits when it is supposed to by incrementing the counter at the end of each iteration. As you can see, there's no difference in how the loop operates. There's still an expression and there's still a body to contain the code to be executed on each iteration of the loop.

Do-While loops

The *do-while* loop is almost identical to the *while* loop with one important difference. The *do-while* loop is guaranteed to execute at least one time, where as a *while* loop is not. For this reason, the condition is placed at the end of the loop instead, so the syntax is slightly different. In fact, the Java documentation states that it is because of the location of the expression that the loop will always execute at least once. No matter which way you look at it, the *do-while* loop **will always execute at least once.**

Let's take a look at it, shall we? let's write a loop that will count from 1 to 10 and then another that has an expression that cannot be true.

```java
int count = 1;
do { //loop 1

    System.out.println(count);

    count++;
} while(count<=10);
int count = 1; //reset counter to 1
do { //loop 2

    System.out.println(count);

    count++;

}
while(1==2); //1 will never be 2 so this is false
```

Now, both of these loop examples do the same thing. They print out the current value of the *count* variable each time the loop executes. The difference being that the second loop has an expression that cannot be true and thus, the loop will not execute **after** the evaluation. Because we are using a *do-while* loop, however, it will execute once. Our expected output for each loop will be:

```
Loop 1:                         Loop 2:
1                               1
2
3
4
5
6
7
8
9
10
```

For loops

for loops differ from the *while* loops that we have looked at previously in that they handle their own counting within the expression. They allow the iteration of code based on a range of values as opposed to whether or not a condition is true. The *for* loop is particularly useful for iterating over arrays or simply repeating a block of code a known number of times.

The syntax of a *for* loop is as follows:

```
for(initialization; termination; increment;) {
    //do stuff here
}
```

That's the general gist of it. Now you may be wondering why there is so much going on where a conditional expression is expected. This is because a *for* loop declares its own counter, its own evaluation and its own increment (or decrement if you want to run a *for* loop backwards).

Here's the good ol' 1-10 example using a *for* loop.

```
for(int count=1; count < 11; count++) {
    System.out.println(count);
}
```

As you can see, we declare and initialize a variable within the *for* loop! Then we have our condition and finally, the increment of the variable. Prior to each iteration of the *for* loop, the condition is evaluated and if it is satisfied, the loop terminates otherwise it will execute. At the end of the code block, the increment takes place. The increment can also be a decrement, as already mentioned, or it can be a specific value such as *count+7*, for example. Then the process repeats until the condition is satisfied.

Traditionally, the *for* loop has been used to iterate over an array. Say you have an integer array with 50 elements within it and you want the summation of all elements within the array. It would be incredibly time consuming and a pain in the ass to have to type what I have typed below:

```
int summation = arr[0] + arr[1] + arr[2] + arr[3] + arr[4]
... + arr[49]
```

That would be very frustrating and a waste of time. With a *for* loop, we can write this instead:

```
int arr[] = new array[50]; //don't forget that this array
                           //currently isn't initialised

int summation = 0;

for(int i=0; i< arr.length; i++) {
    summation += arr[i];
}

    System.out.println(summation);
```

This makes these scenarios so much easier. However, unless you specifically require the numeric value of the iteration, Java has a better solution known as the *enhanced for* loop or *for-each* loop. Read on below.

For each loops (enhanced *for* loops)

The *for-each* loop is the newer style *for* loop that is much more elegant. You don't need to use it, the old style *for* is perfectly fine. But you should at least be familiar with it in case you see it somewhere else. It's better to be prepared.

The *for-each* loop simply says "for each item, x, in list y..." and proceeds to iterate through the list until it reaches the end. This does away with the need to know the length of the list and the need to keep track of the current iteration if the loop. The only real downside is that if you need to know the iteration, you will have to add a counter such as that seen with the *while* loop.

A typical *for-each* loop looks like this, imagining the array *arr* that I previously demonstrated above exists here:

```java
for (int i : arr) {
    System.out.println(i);
}
```

Now this *for-each* loop does exactly the same as the *for* loop shown previous but it's so much neater. It reads as "for each integer *i* in the array *arr*...". For each iteration of the loop, *i* takes on the value stored in the element of the array *arr* at the current index. We then access that value by referring to *i* and using *System.out.println()* to print the value to a new line in the console.

Infinite loops

Infinite loops are exactly what they sound like, loops that loop for infinity. It's quite easy to accidentally create an infinite loop. Nothing particularly catastrophic happens if you do, it'll just cause your program to hang and become unresponsive until it eventually dies when your OS realises it's not listening anymore. If you don't want that to happen, make sure your loops can terminate. This isn't so much of an issue with a *for* loop because, unless you create an infinite loop on purpose, the termination condition should be written within the signature of the *for* loop.

I'm sure that's got you curious, can you create a *for* loop without an *initialization, termination* or *increment*? The answer is yes. You can omit any or all parts of the *for* loop signature. I've never had a reason to do this but if you decide to do so, be sure to give a means for the loop to exit.

```java
int i = 0;
for(;;) {
    i++;
    if(i>10) break;
}
```

This is an example of an infinite *for* loop with the ability to exit itself at some point, when *i>10* in this example. The *break* keyword will exit any loop, as discussed below.

Finally, in regards to infinite loops, as you've seen with the *while* loop, the code within the loop must manipulate the variable within the expression of the loop in order to make that expression evaluate to false at some point, thus terminating the loop. If this does not happen, an infinite loop is born!

Nested Loops

Nested loops are something you should know about but I don't want to go into too much detail about them. They are simply loops within loops. You may create as many as you wish, think of the movie Inception. Nesting *for* loops is a common practice when iterating over multi-dimensional arrays, for example. Or to create a grid within a 2D game. Nested loops don't have to be of the same type. You can have a *for* loop inside a *while* loop and vice versa.

The following code demonstrates a nested *for* loop:

```java
for (int i=0; i< 10; i++) {
    for (int j = 0; j < 10; j++)
    {
        System.out.println("i=" + i + ", j=" + j);
    }
}
```

This code will print out the value of *i* and *j* at each iteration of each loop. This means we can expect to see i=0, j=0, i=0, j=1, i=0, j=2 etc until both *i* and *j* reach 9. For each iteration of the outer loop, the inner loop will run its full 10 iterations.

Break and Continue

There are two Java keywords that you will find very useful when working with loops. They are the *break* and *continue* keywords. We have already seen the *break* keyword demonstrated in this chapter, it essentially says to the containing loop "Stop right here, we're done" and the loop terminates at the point that the keyword is encountered. The *continue* keyword is similar but instead of saying "we're done" it says "Stop here, start a new iteration". It terminates only the current iteration of a loop and initiates the next iteration. Both keywords terminate the loop at the point that they are encountered so if there is any code below them, it won't be executed.

Key Points

1. There are 4 types of loop: The *while*, *do-while*, *for* and *for-each*
2. The *for-each* loop is a newer version of the *for* loop
3. *while* loops are easy to end up infinite
4. *for* loops keep track of the number of iterations, *while* loops do not
5. *break* and *continue* help to control the flow of your loops
6. Nested loops can contain a mixture of types of loop

Exercises

1. Write a *for* loop that starts at 1 and ends at 10 which prints out the first 10 numbers of a triangle sequence starting at 1. The formula for this sequence is n = n(n+1)/2
2. Change your *for* loop to a *while* loop
3. Write a *for* loop which achieves the same result with:
    a. no initialisation, just a termination and increment
    b. no termination, just an initialisation and increment
    c. no increment, just an initialisation and termination
    d. **only** an initialisation
    e. **only** a termination
    f. **only** an increment
    g. no initialisation, termination or increment
4. Declare an integer array with 10 elements and use a *for* loop to initialize each element and then use a *for-each* loop to cycle through each element of the array
5. Write any loop that prints from 1 to 10 but skips all even numbers. *Hint: use the modulo operator; [even number] % 2 = 0*

Chapter 7: Functions
What is a function?

Functions, also called methods and less frequently routines, are reusable blocks of code which can be written once and called from anywhere within your code. We've already been using a function, *main()*. But that's not really something we have a choice over, it's kind of essential and we can't go invoking the *main()* method whenever we want to. A function is a core part of programming because it aids readability by segmenting your code, increases efficiency because you're not rewriting the same code over and over again and subtly emphasizes the DRY (Don't Repeat Yourself!) ideology.

Functions will serve any purpose you write them for. When writing a program, you should take a step back and look at everything you need to do such as "ask a user for their name", "generate a random String", "sort an array" etc. All tasks within a program can be broken down and segmented into functions.

When you write a function, it's header is typically referred to as its signature. The *main()* function signature, for example, is:

```
void main(String[] args)
```

and this means that you can't go and create another function with the same signature - the name *main* and one argument of the type *String[]*.

The syntax of a function in Java is as follows:

```
access-modifier return-type name(parameters) {
    //code here
}
```

An average function may look something like this:

```
int giveMeANumber() {
    return 10;
}
```

or

```
void sayHello() {
    System.out.println("Hello");
}
```

You don't have to explicitly provide an access modifier, please refer to chapter 4 on Access Modifiers for more information on this. You do, however, have to provide a return type when declaring a function. The return type indicates whether or not the function should return any data and if so, what type of data will be returned. You can use any of the primitive types described in Chapter 3 as a return type or *void* if you do not need to return any data. Notice in the first example above, *giveMeANumber()*, within the body of the function there is a statement - *return 10; return* is a keyword which, when encountered, will exit the function and return the data that follows. If your function is not of type *void* then it **must** have a return statement. You can use the *return* keyword on its own to exit a function of type *void* but it is not required. When returning a value, it is returned to where the function is called.

```
private int giveMeANumber() {
    return 10;
}

int number = giveMeANumber();
```

As you can see here, to call a function we simply write its name where we want to call it. When the machine interprets this piece of code, it will refer to the function and execute the code therein and then return to the point it was at and continue execution.

Parameters/Arguments

Sometimes, we might want to give a function some data to work with and to do this we use parameters, also referred to as arguments. We can give a function as many or as few arguments as necessary and their type helps to determine the signature of a function. We've already seen arguments with the *main()* function but let's create some of our own.

```
int multiplyBy(int number, int multiplier) {
    return (number*multiplier);
}
```

This integer function will take two integers, multiply them and then return the result. Remember the little section on variable scope within chapter 3? Now is the time to bring that to the forefront of your mind.

Let's say we have a program that has a variable called *number* and another called *multiplier* which are to be passed to the above function which also uses the same variable names.

```
class ScopeDemo {

    //visible to the whole program
    static int number=0;
    static int multiplier=0;

    static int multiplyBy(int number, int multiplier) {
        //local variables number, multiplier
        return (number*multiplier);
    }

    public static void main(String[] args) {
        number = 10;
        multiplier = 10;

        System.out.println(multiplyBy(number,
                                      multiplier));

    }

} //end class
```

Firstly, please ignore the *static* keyword for now. So this program will print out *100* which is, hopefully, what you'd expect. What if we changed our code to look like this:

```
class ScopeDemo {

    //visible to the whole program, global variables
    static int number=0;
    static int multiplier=0;

    static int multiplyBy(int number, int multiplier) {
        //local variables number, multiplier
        return (number*multiplier);
    }

    public static void main(String[] args) {
        number = 10;
        multiplier = 10;

        System.out.println(multiplyBy(8, 10));
    }

} //end class
```

Doing this, you'll see that the output is 80 and the *multiplyBy()* function doesn't even touch the global *multiplier* and *number* variables. This is because, variables declared within a function (including as parameters) are visible only to that function. Despite having the same names, this remains true. If we wanted to access the global variables within a function that has variables of the same name then we would have to make use of the *dot notation* like so:

```
class ScopeDemo {

    //visible to the whole program, global variables
    static int number=10;
    static int multiplier=10;

    static int multiplyBy(int number, int multiplier) {
        //local variables number, multiplier
        return
(ScopeDemo.number*ScopeDemo.multiplier);
    }

    public static void main(String[] args) {
```

```
        System.out.println(multiplyBy(8, 10));
    }

} //end class
```

This change in the code causes the *multiplyBy()* function to refer directly to the global variables instead with the use of dot notation. This causes the output of the *multiplyBy()* method to be 100 regardless of what values are passed to it. ScopeDemo.*number* says "get the variable *number* from the class *ScopeDemo*". This is atypical of OOP, though. In chapter 12 we will look at objects and the *this* keyword as an alternative solution to this problem.

Overloading

Overloading is a term used to describe multiple functions with the same name but different signatures. Also referred to as method overloading or function overloading. In some cases it will just create confusion but there are also situations where it's a very useful technique. Such as when you want to provide a method that performs a calculation but you're not sure whether the argument will be an *integer* or a *float* so you cater for both instances. See the code snippet below for an example:

```
class ScopeDemo {

    //visible to the whole program, global variables
    static int num1=10;
    static float num2=10.1F;

    static int multiplyBy(int number) {
        //local variables number, multiplier
        return (number*10);
    }

    static float multiplyBy(float number) {
        return (number*10);
    }
```

```
    public static void main(String[] args) {

        System.out.println("int: " +
                            multiplyBy(num1));

        System.out.println("float: " +
                            multiplyBy(num2));

    }

} //end class
```

Go ahead and type out this code, compile and run it. Your expected
output is:

```
int: 100
float: 101.0
```

The program should compile and run without any issues at all, despite
having two functions with the same name. This is the beauty of function
overloading. We have two functions here both called *multiplyBy()* but
they are not of the same return type, although they could be (refer to
type casting in chapter 3 and see the following code for an example).
They also have the same number of arguments, the only difference being
the argument type. It is the difference in the argument data type that
makes the function signature different which in turn allows us to create
overloaded functions.

This code snippet demonstrates the same concept as previous but
instead of returning a *float*, the second *multiplyBy()* method returns an
integer in the same way that the first does. It still takes a *float* as its
argument, however. The result is cast from a *float* to an *integer*.

```
class ScopeDemo {

    //visible to the whole program, global variables
    static int num1=10;
    static float num2=10.1F;

    static int multiplyBy(int number) {
```

```
        //local variables number, multiplier
        return (number*10);
    }

    static int multiplyBy(float number) {
        return (int)(number*10); //cast float to int
    }

    public static void main(String[] args) {

        System.out.println("int: " +
                            multiplyBy(num1));

        System.out.println("float(int): " +
                            multiplyBy(num2));
    }
} //end class
```

Key Points

1. Consider how you can break your program up into functions before writing your code
2. functions must have a return type
3. functions do not **need** an *access modifier* but you can specify one if you need to
4. functions not of the *void* return type must return some data
5. data is returned to the point where the function is called
6. you can have functions with the same name as long as the parameters are not of the same type

Chapter 8: Intermission

So after cramming a load of knowledge into your head, I figured it was time to take a timeout from new stuff just for a while. Instead, we're going to put together all we've learned so far to use and make an interactive console application. There will be a thing or two that's new here but they'll be explained in the coming chapters. We're going to, or I'm going to and you're going to copy and play with, write a program that asks the user what they want to do and then provide 2 options - convert a temperature to degrees Celsius or to degrees Fahrenheit. A pretty basic program as far as programming goes, it was one of the first real programs I wrote whilst learning and thoroughly enjoyed the process of and so I hope you feel the same.

Without further ado, let us begin!

```java
import java.util.Scanner;

class IntermissionOne {

    //Create a scanner object to handle user input
    static Scanner in = new Scanner(System.in);

    //main entry point method
    public static void main(String[] args) {

        System.out.println("Simple Temperature
                            Converter\n");
        getUserInput();
    }

    //convert fahrenheit f to celsius
    // temp (c) = (temp (f) - 32) x (5/9)
    static double toCelsius(double f) {
        double celsius = (f - 32d) * (5d/9d);
        return celsius;
    }

    //convert celsius to farhenheit
    // temp (f) = ((temp (c) x (9/5)) + 32
    static double toFahrenheit(double c) {
```

```java
        double fahrenheit = (c * (9d/5d)) + 32d;
        return fahrenheit;
}

static void getUserInput() {
    //ask user for a choice and give them appropriate
                                             options
    System.out.println("\nPlease choose an option:");
    System.out.println("1) Celsius to Fahrenheit");
    System.out.println("2) Fahrenheit to Celsius");
    System.out.println("0) Exit");

    //wait for / get user input
    String input = in.nextLine();

    //store users integer input
    int switcher=0;

    double temp = 0d;

    //store whether or not theres been an error
    boolean hasError = false;

    //try and convert the user input to an integer
    try {
        switcher = Integer.parseInt(input);
    }
    //catch any errors that may arise from
                                    Integer.parseInt()
    catch(NumberFormatException nfe) {
        hasError = true;
        nfe.printStackTrace();
    }
    catch(NullPointerException npe) {
        hasError = true;
        npe.printStackTrace();
    }

    if(hasError) {
        //recall the method if there is an error
        System.out.println("Your input was not
                    numeric. Please choose again.");
        getUserInput(); //take note of this
```

```java
        }
    else
    {
        switch(switcher) {
            case 1: //convert celsius to fahrenheit

                input = in.nextLine();

                temp = getDoubleFromUserStr(input);


                if( Double.isNaN(temp) ) {
                    //recall the method if there is an
                                                error
                    System.out.println("Your input was
            not numeric. Please choose again.");
                    getUserInput(); //take note of
                                            this
                }
                else {
                    System.out.println(temp + "
celsius in fahrenheit is " + toFahrenheit(temp) );
                    getUserInput(); //take note of
                                            this
                }

            break;

            case 2: //convert fahrenheit to celsius
                input = in.nextLine();

                temp = getDoubleFromUserStr(input);


                if( Double.isNaN(temp) ) {
                    //recall the method if there is an
                                                error
                    System.out.println("Your input was
            not numeric. Please choose again.");
                    getUserInput(); //take note of
                                                this
                }
                else {
```

```
                            System.out.println(temp + "
    fahrenheit in celsius is " + toCelsius(temp) );
                    getUserInput(); //take note of
                                            this

                }

            break;

            case 0: //exit the program
                System.out.println("Goodbye!");
                System.exit(0);
            break;

            default:
                System.out.println("Your choice was
            not recognised. Please try again");
                getUserInput(); //take note of this
            break;
        } //end switch
    } //end else
} //end getUserInput()

static double getDoubleFromUserStr(String str) {
    double temp = 0d;
    //try and convert the user input to an integer
    try {
        temp = Double.parseDouble(str);
    }
    //catch any errors that may arise from
                                Double.parseDouble()
    catch(NumberFormatException nfe) {
        nfe.printStackTrace();
        return Double.NaN;
    }
    catch(NullPointerException npe) {
        npe.printStackTrace();
        return Double.NaN;
    }

    return temp;
    }
} //end class
```

Now this is a pretty big leap from variables, conditionals, loops and functions. We've made use of all but loops here, and then some! The first thing you'll notice with this code is its long! Well its 140~ lines so nothing too strenuous, I hope. But let's dissect, if you're ready.

The very first line of code up there before we even begin the class is this:

```
import java.util.Scanner;
```

This tells the compiler to import the *java.util.Scanner;* class. This is our first real taste of objects! After we open our class, we encounter this line:

```
static Scanner in = new Scanner(System.in);
```

This is the instantiation of an object, it creates a copy of the *Scanner* class for us to make use of. We'll take a more in-depth look at objects when we hit Chapter 12 but for now, just know what's going on. Instantiation means to create an instance of.

Next we get our *main()* method, I won't talk too much about that. Just note that we only have 2 lines of code in there.

We then encounter four methods, the first two, *toCelsius()* and *toFahrenheit()* both take a *double* and return the converted result. If you look inside these methods, they declare and initialize a *double* variable with the relevant equation. The important thing here is that all *integer* numbers in this equation are preceded by the letter **d**. This is so Java interprets those whole numbers as *doubles* as opposed to *integers*. If we don't do this, Java will treat them as *integers* and our calculations won't work. Try and write a quick program to print out the value of a *double* with the value of (9/5) then change it to (9d/5d) to see what I mean!

Next we have the *getUserInput()* method. I'll go through that last as it's the longest so let's discuss the *getDoubleFromUserStr()* method first. This method takes a *String* value and attempts to convert it to a *double* then return it. If it cannot do this, we use the Double wrapper class to access a *constant double* which holds a Not-a-Number value and we return this instead. Please note that the Double wrapper class is not the same as the *double* primitive data type! You'll see we use this class to attempt to convert our *String* to a *double* too. The code contained within the *getDoubleFromUserStr()* method is encapsulated within a *try-catch* block. This is a really important concept for error handling and we'll look into it more in Chapter 13. Just know that certain code can throw *exceptions* and they need to be handled, so we try this certain code and catch any *exceptions* it throws. If we don't do this, our program will run fine until it encounters one of these *exceptions* and then it'll crash and exit. Not very pretty for the end user. I feel it's also important to note that this *getDoubleFromUserStr()* method was not in my initial program, I decided to add it to reduce the amount of overall code I had. You'll see that this method is called twice, I initially had the code that's inside the method at both locations, it's always good to improve your code to adhere to the DRY (Don't repeat yourself) principle.

Finally, the *getUserInput()* method. This method prints out several lines of text to the user to ask them to choose an option. It then calls the *nextLine()* method of our *in* variable, which is an instance of the *Scanner* class. This is OOP. Again, there'll be more on this in Chapter 12. When this method is called, the program waits for the user to give input before continuing, it'll wait for as long as it has to. We declare a couple of local variables that'll be useful to store the *integral* value of the user input so we can use it in our *switch* statement, a *double* to store the temperature the user wishes to convert and a *boolean* to act as a flag if we encounter any errors within the *try-catch* block we use when attempting to convert the user input into an *integer*. That's quite a mouthful. My bad.

Right, after our *try-catch* block has ran, we check if the *boolean* is set to true (this'll happen in the *try-catch* if any *exceptions* are caught). If so, we tell the user about the problem and then we call the method again. You'll notice on this line that there's a comment which says **take note of this**. This is because calling a function **from within itself** is known as **recursion** and we'll be taking a closer look at this in the next chapter. If there is no error, we get right into our *switch* statement.

There are four cases in our *switch*, 0, 1, 2 and default. Case 0 calls *System.exit(0)* which gracefully terminates the program. Cases 1 and 2 both call the *nextLine()* method of our Scanner object and then attempt to convert that input to a *double* by calling our *getDoubleFromUserStr()* method. If the returned value is equal to *Double.isNan()*, which is a method of the Double wrapper class that identifies *doubles* with a value of Not-a-Number, then the user is informed and the *getUserInput()* method calls itself again. More recursion! Otherwise, the user is told of the result of the conversion by including a call to the relevant conversion method within the *System.out.println()* call and then the *getUserInput()* method is called again to reinitiate the cycle.

If you're new to programming, this will seem like a hell of a lot to take in at once so don't be frustrated at yourself if you have to re-read some stuff or can't grasp a particular concept right away, especially if it's the stuff we are yet to examine. The amount of times I have re-read whole chapters just to get a better grasp on something are beyond counting. Not to mention the time I spend referring to the documentation of a language I am working with. That's an important thing, by the way, I never once read a book that said that it's ok to find yourself looking at documentation frequently, all the while I self-taught, and it wasn't until I went to university that I learned that this was the norm.

But, if you feel like you've got this down, great!

Try and write this program on your own without copying the code. All you need to know are the formulae which follow below. There is no solution at the back of the book for this one, every programmer is different and there are countless ways for any one problem to be solved so it's always good to explore your own path!

Celsius to Fahrenheit :

$$°F = (°C \times (9 \div 5)) + 32$$

Fahrenheit to Celsius:

$$°C = (°F - 32) \times (5 \div 9)$$

Don't forget that *double* values should be followed with a **d**.

Chapter 9: Recursion

Recursion. Google "recursion" =) Seriously, though, give it a go.

Anyway, recursion. The technical computing-related definition is a method where the solution to a problem depends on solutions to smaller instances of the same problem.

What I know as recursion is the act of calling a method from within itself. An algorithmic approach would be more beneficial of recursion than, say, my example in Chapter 8 but that's still recursion nonetheless.

Let's take a look at the classic recursion example in programming - calculating the nth Fibonacci number. This isn't the most practical example of recursion, though, so we'll take a look at some other stuff too but first, get this in a .java file and compile it for your own satisfaction.

```java
class Fib {

    public static void main(String[] args) {
        for(int i=0; i<11; i++)
            System.out.println(fibN(i));
    }

    static int fibN(int n) {
        if(n <= 1) {
            return n;
        }
        else {
            return fibN(n-1) + fibN(n-2);
        }
    }
}
```

So, that's it. We create our Fib class and get a loop rolling in our main method to output the result of our *fibN()* method 11 times for the 0-10th Fibonacci term.

The *fibN()* method will return the value of n if it is less than or equal to 1, this is because the first term of the Fibonacci sequence is 1. Well, it's technically zero but that's also the 0th term so it doesn't count. Zero will return zero, -1 will return -1 and so on. If *n* is greater than one, however, the recursion begins. If the value of *n* is 2 then the value returned will be the value of *fibN(1)+fibN(0)* which is 1. If the value of *n* is 3 then the following will take place:

return *fibN(2)* + *fibN(1)*

fibN(2) = *fibN(1)* + *fibN(0)*

fibN(1) = 1
fibN(0) = 0

fibN(1) = 1

Thus making the final result 2.

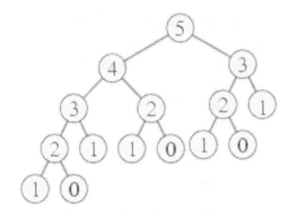

The tree above shows the recursive process for computing *fibN(5)*. Working our way down from the top, the initial call to *fibN(5)* is at the very top. This invokes calls to *fibN(4)* and *fibN(3)* which therefore invoke calls to *fibN(3)* and *fibN(2)*, *fibN(2)* and *fibN(1)* respectively and so on until the value passed to *fibN()* is less than or equal to one at which point the recursive process is finished and the final result is returned.

Where does the data go for each recursive call? Using 3 as our example because it has less recursive calls, when the method is called, the ensuing steps take place:

```
In order, A-E.

call to (A) fibN(3)

        (A) step one fibN(3) = (B) fibN(2) + (E) fibN(1)
        (B) step two fibN(2) = (C) fibN(1) + (D) fibN(0)
        (E) step three fibN(1) = fibN(1)

        (B) step two fibN(2) = 1 + 0. Step two is finished
        and returns '1'  to step one, A.

        (E) step three fibN(1) = 1. Step three is finished
        and returns '1'  to step one, A.

        A makes a call to B which makes a call to C and D
        then B is   completed so E can complete and finally
        A can return its result.
```

What I'm trying to portray above is that the recursive functions execute in the order that they are encountered so when A is called, it calls B and E and A cannot complete until B and E have completed execution. I don't want to over complicate things but this aims to show that the data is passed back through each recursive call until it reaches the first call to *fibN()* and is then able to provide a result.

Ok, take a quick breather. I almost lost myself writing that, hopefully you're still with me!

Now let's look at a more practical example of recursion, something that'll be more beneficial. The Fibonacci recursion above is bad. It's a great example, but it's not efficient for the task so it's just an example. You'd be better off computing each number up to *n* instead of running *fibN()* n-1 times because it'll be a lot less costly on computer power. Not that it's a huge deal in this day and age but the principles of optimisation are always good to bear in mind. In fact, we'll take both of these tasks and time each execution in a future chapter to see the difference in performance!

We can use recursion for things such as sorting data lists by whatever criteria we specify, finding the maximum number in a list of numbers, solving Sudoku (although I've never tried), navigating binary trees, calculating factorials, solving mazes or many other uses. I was going to use a couple of sorting algorithms that demonstrate recursion but they are a bit beyond the scope of an Introduction to Java book plus the bulk of the algorithm takes the focus away from the recursion so I'll be whipping up a method to identify the largest number in a list of numbers instead.

```java
class LargestNumber {

    public static void main(String[] args) {

        //99 random numbers courtesy of random.org
        int [] numbers = {
            9,11,85,41,97,35,44,29,
            54,49,14,78,32,59,23,77,
            54,19,93,93,3,67,51,82,49,
            61,76,28,46,50,72,6,40,73,
            66,10,49,56,17,95,29,2,75,
            60,52,11,19,79,48,55,8,21,
            44,33,67,17,51,12,46,92,79,
            55,4,72,62,47,62,85,20,27,49,
            6,18,77,33,72,50,63,74,44,75,
            69,80,74,82,55,7,25,92,70,41,
            28,8,57,55,14,50,66,48};

        //print result of findMax() method
        System.out.println( findMax( numbers, 0 ) );

    } //end main()


    static int findMax(int[] n, int offset) {

        //at end of array
        if(n.length-1 == offset) {
            return n[offset];
        }
        else {
            //get max of n and findmax()
```

```
        return Math.max(n[offset], findMax(n,
offset+1) );
        }
    }
}
```

This code takes an *integer array* of 99 numbers and identifies the largest number among them. The *findMax()* method is recursive and is where the magic happens. We look at one element of the given array and if it is the last element, we return the value. If it is not the last element, we call a method that is part of the **Math** class called *max()* which will return the higher of 2 numbers, we then return that result. The numbers we provide are the current element we are looking at and the next element of which the value is acquired by calling the *findMax()* method again. This process repeats, like Inception, until we are left with an answer.

There's a tonne of stuff on the internet about recursion so if there's not enough here to wrap your head around it then I implore you to take a look online. Your programming skill will improve no end with a good understanding of recursion under your belt. But rest assured, I don't think there's any further need for it through the rest of this book!

Chapter 10: ArrayList

I couldn't decide where exactly was the best place to discuss ArrayList's so I decided to just squeeze in a chapter about them somewhere around the middle. The reason I have decided to include this short chapter is because I will be using the ArrayList class in future chapters so you need to know about them. They are also kind of useful, so you need to know about them.

An ArrayList, in Java, is an ordered collection of data which can be thought of as a *dynamic array*. It can be considered an array that **is not of fixed length**. Another way of looking at is to call it a resizable-array implementation of the List interface, and thus you should also consider looking into *List* and ***Collection*** which I won't be covering here. The length of an ArrayList can change by adding and removing elements at runtime which is not possible with a normal array.

When you declare a normal array:

```
int [] arr = new int[10];
```

You also declare how many elements the array will contain; this is to allow the Java Runtime System to allocate the appropriate amount of memory for the array. There will be situations when you don't know how many elements an array will need, keeping track of connected clients within a server, for example, and this is where the ArrayList will shine.

Unlike the arrays you are familiar with already, you declare an ArrayList like so:

```
ArrayList<Object Type> listName = new ArrayList<Object Type>();
```

This is quite a strange concept at first, using the angle brackets (chevrons) like that and such. We replace *Object Type* with the type of object that will be stored in our ArrayList. Yes, objects will be stored as opposed to primitive data. That means if we want to store integers, for example, we would use the *Integer* object as opposed to the *int* primitive type. You can, however, use primitive arrays (e.g. *int[]*) as your object type. This also means we can store objects of our own in an ArrayList which is good news for us! Similarly to a normal array, the ArrayList does have indices to access the data, but we access it differently:

```
listName.get(index);
```

We call the *get()* method of the ArrayList and pass it an index as a parameter. There are several implementations of the *get()* method and you should study them in the Java documentation. We add data to the ArrayList in the same way:

```
listName.add(Object of appropriate type);
```

We are calling the *add()* method of the ArrayList and passing it an object.

You don't have to specify the type of data that your ArrayList will store but it's good practice to do so and the compiler will throw you a warning if you don't. It ensures that you don't accidentally store the wrong kind of data in your ArrayList.

Let's take a look at a working example, shall we?

To use the ArrayList you must import the appropriate package:

```
import java.util.ArrayList;
```

We then create a test class of some kind, I'll just name the class *Chapter10* for lack of a better name. Here's what the complete *Chapter10.java* code looks like:

```java
import java.util.ArrayList;

class Chapter10 {
    static ArrayList<String> list1 = new
                                ArrayList<String>();
    static ArrayList list2 = new ArrayList();
    static ArrayList list3;

    public static void main(String[] args) {
        String s1 = "string 1";
        System.out.println("adding s1 to list1");
        list1.add(s1);
        System.out.println("adding s1 to list 2");
        list2.add(s1);
        System.out.println("adding 10 to list 2");
        list2.add(10);
        System.out.println("adding new string to list
                                                2");
        list2.add(new String("string 2"));
        //System.out.println("adding s1 to list3");
        //list3.add(s1);

        System.out.print("List 1:");
        for(String s : list1) {
            System.out.print(" " + s);
        }
        System.out.println("");
        System.out.print("List 2:");
        for(Object o : list2) {
            if(o instanceof String) {
                String s = (String) o;
                System.out.print(" " + s);
            }

            if(o instanceof Integer) {
                int i = (Integer) o;
                System.out.print(" " + i);
            }
        }
        System.out.println(list2.get(list2.size()-1));

    }
}
```

Alrighty, get that typed up and compiled before going any further. There's some new stuff in there along with some good and bad practice which I'll discuss now.

First of all, you'll notice the three ArrayList declarations:

```
static ArrayList<String> list1 = new
                               ArrayList<String>();
static ArrayList list2 = new ArrayList();
static ArrayList list3;
```

list1 will store String objects only, *list2* will store anything (e.g. String objects, integers, Dinosaur objects etc) and list3 is not initialised.

You should always use the first style of declaration and initialisation, this ensures that you don't accidentally store the wrong type of object in your ArrayList (which will cause all kinds of headache in the future when it comes to handling the data) and will result in compiler errors if you try to assign data of the incorrect type to the ArrayList. The second type of declaration doesn't specify a type so we can store whatever we want in this ArrayList, this means we need to assess what kind of data is coming out of the ArrayList when we access it. "Generic Lists" is a good starting point if you want to learn more about storing data of an unknown type within a List of some kind, but that goes beyond the scope of this chapter and this book. Finally, *list3* will cause a compilation error if you try to do anything with it because it's not initialised. Uncomment the commented out code within the above example to see the result of this so you're familiar with the event.

Next up, we have our *main()* method. In here we print out a line each time we do something so we know what is taking place, but for now let's remove those lines to focus on analysing what is happening with the ArrayLists:

```
String s1 = "string 1";
list1.add(s1);
```

90

```
list2.add(s1);
list2.add(10);
list2.add(new String("string 2"));

for(String s : list1) {
    System.out.print(" " + s);
}
for(Object o : list2) {
    if(o instanceof String) {
        String s = (String) o;
        System.out.print(" " + s);
    }

    if(o instanceof Integer) {
        int i = (Integer) o;
        System.out.print(" " + i);
    }
}
```

We create a *String* variable at first, don't forget that a *String* is actually an object that is treated as a primitive data type by Java. This is just to save us having to repeat a string each time we add something to an ArrayList. The next two lines add this string to ArrayList *list1* and *list2*. Next, we just add an *integer* value of 10 to *list2*. **This is an important point**:- our *list2* ArrayList now contains both a String object and an Integer object because *list2* does not define the type of data that will be stored within it. Finally, we add another *String* to *list2* but this time we create a new *String* object on the fly by using the *new* keyword followed by the constructor of the String class which takes a string as a parameter.

Next, you'll see a *for* loop which uses the *foreach* syntax to iterate over each element within the *list1* ArrayList. Each element of *list1* is printed on a single line, separated by a space. Not ideal for strings but I'm trying to keep the code short! Finally, there's a second *for* loop. This time, there are a couple of *if* statements inside. Again, **this is an important point**:- the *if* statements use the keyword *instanceof* which compares object types, if both the left and right hand operands are of the same type, the comparison will equal true, otherwise false. The *instanceof* keyword would perhaps be better thought of as an operator, it's essentially the comparison operator (==) for objects. So, in the example above, this is used to determine whether the object is a String or Integer, if so, the object is cast to the appropriate type (this means to convert it from *Object* to *String*, for example) and then the value is printed out.

```
int i = (Integer) o;
```

This is the casting of *Object o* to *int i* using the *Integer* object.

Within this final *for* loop, if there are no matches for the current object being assessed then the loop will just overlook it, because there is no code to handle an object of unknown type, and move on to the next object within the ArrayList.

Finally, the last line of code within our *main()* method is this:

```
System.out.println(list2.get(list2.size()-1));
```

This says to print out the last value stored within the *list2* ArrayList. Now, this will throw an *ArrayIndexOutOfBoundsException* if the *list2* ArrayList is empty, otherwise it will always print out the value stored therein. The important bit here is to observe the use of the *get()* method of an ArrayList. Also, just in case you overlooked it, the *size()* method returns the number of elements within an ArrayList. We then subtract 1 from this value because ArrayList indices are zero based and so 10 elements would mean the last index is 9; *size()* would return 10, the final index would be 9 (*size()-1*).

Hopefully this provides you with a nice, clear understanding of how to use the ArrayList when you need one. If you find yourself confused with the concept, head on over to the online Java documentation and study their content in a hope that it can shed some more light on the topic for you!

Chapter 11: Static

You may have noticed that the *static* keyword is everywhere. But what does it mean? If something is *static* then it can only exist once. Or at least that's how I look at it. Members declared as static will only exist **once** within a program no matter how many instances of the class exist. So if you had a class called *Dinosaur* and it had a static variable called *legs* then, no matter if you have 1 or 100 instances of the class *Dinosaur*, there will only be **one instance of** the variable *legs* that is shared between all the *Dinosaur* classes.

In a nutshell, static members belong to a class instead of a specific instance. A big pain in the ass when writing small test modules, for example, where you want a couple of global variables available to you within the *main()* method is needing to declare those variables as static. This is because the very characteristics of a static member mean that a static method can only access static variables. You can also access non-static members within a static method if done through an instantiated object, of course. We'll see more on instantiation in the next chapter.

Anyway, quickly moving on. I just wanted to touch on *static* because it's seldom ever mentioned and you'll forever wonder why you can't access non-static variables from your *main()* method otherwise!

Chapter 12: Classes

What is a Class?

As you've seen so far, every program we write in Java is contained within a class, it's fair to say we've been writing our own classes. But not every class has to contain a *main()* method and not every class is a program. Most classes, in fact, serve to break down programming problems into smaller chunks and that's where Object-Oriented Programming comes in. From here on out we'll begin to define and write our own classes using the knowledge we have learned from the previous chapters.

When planning a program, we have to look at the problems that require a solution. We then break these problems down into smaller chunks to segment our program. When working from an OOP angle, we want to identify any and everything that could represent an object in reality. A prime example of this would be a simple game in which animals exist. We'd want an object for each type of animal. Or, a banking system may have an object for the customer, another for the customer account etc. Every object we can conceive will be represented by a class.

The key point you should take away from this is that classes represent objects.

Defining a Class

To define a class, we use the same syntax that we have up until now. We choose a name for our class and proceed to create it like so:

Class Definition

```
class ClassName {

}
```

This is an empty class called *ClassName* which would be contained within a file called *ClassName.java*. Then we have variables. These are declared as usual too. But now is the time we start making use of access modifiers. For now, we'll treat everything as *private*.

Declaring Variables

```
class ClassName {

    private int var1;
    private int var2;

}
```

I've added two variables to the *ClassName* class called *var1* and *var2*, both *integers* which are yet to be initialized. Next, let's add a method. Variables within a class are sometimes referred to as member variables.

Class Constructor

```
class ClassName {

    private int var1;
    private int var2;

    public ClassName() {
        var1 = 0;
        var2 = 0;
    }

}
```

This is an awesome feature of classes. The class constructor. Notice that the method we added has the same name as the class? That makes it the class constructor. Equally as important, however, is that this method is **public** and it has **no return type**.

The purpose of the class constructor is to execute whenever a class is instantiated; whenever an instance (copy) of the class is made to be used as an object that it represents within a program. Remember, instantiation means to create an instance of. The constructor executes automatically and is used to prepare the class for use such as by initiating variables, being given data etc. **Note:** If no class constructor is provided, an empty constructor will be automatically created at compile-time.

We can also overload a class constructor so we can have more than one version of it. Remember the discussion on function signatures in Chapter 7, regarding overloading? The same applies here.

Overloading the Constructor

```
class ClassName {

    private int var1;
    private int var2;

    public ClassName() {
        var1 = 0;
        var2 = 0;
    }

    public ClassName(int var1, int var2) {
        this.var1 = var1;
        this.var2 = var2;
    }

}
```

Here we've added another constructor method, this time it takes 2 *integer* arguments and then assigns them to the *integer* variables *var1* and *var2* that we created at the beginning of our class.

The *this* keyword

Notice the *this* keyword. This is super useful when working with classes. It basically means "this class". So, when we use it here, we're effectively saying

```
ClassName.var1 = var1
ClassName.var2 = var2
```

where *var1* and *var2* are the values provided as arguments. This could be rewritten so we don't have to use the *this* keyword but that's not quite as fun.

```
class ClassName {
    private int var1;
    private int var2;
    public ClassName() {
        var1 = 0;
        var2 = 0;
    }
    public ClassName(int v1, int v2) {
        var1 = v1;
        var2 = v2;
    }
}
```

Our variables are now initiated upon the instantiation of our class, great! But, how do we access them if they are set to *private*? Well, we could change the access modifier to *public* but that's not a good idea. What if the values are important enough to ensure they aren't accidentally changed when accessing them? We'll keep it *private* for that reason for now.

The solution to this dilemma is to create a *public* method that allows manipulation of the variables. We do this by creating methods that are commonly known as *getter* and *setter* methods which *get* and *set* variables respectively.

```
class ClassName {

    private int var1;
    private int var2;

    public ClassName() {
        var1 = 0;
        var2 = 0;
    }

    public ClassName(int var1, int var2) {
        this.var1 = var1;
        this.var2 = var2;
    }

    public int getVar1() {
        return var1;
    }

    public int getVar2() {
        return var2;
    }

    public void setVar1(int value) {
        this.var1 = value;
    }
}
```

There you have it, *getter* and *setter* methods for our class. Notice that there is no *setter* method for *var2*. This is to emphasize that *private* variables don't **need** to have a *setter* method. We can just provide a *getter* method to allow access to the variable. It's important to note here that *getter* and *setter* methods are not part of the functionality of Java, they are just methods that perform the task of getting or setting a variable and thus they are referred to as *getters* and *setters* but there is nothing unique or special about them. They aren't even required unless you require the functionality!

Instantiating our Class

Ok, now we have a pretty robust demonstrative class. Sure, it has no real purpose but to illustrate the creation of a class but it is a class and we need to test it out. That's what we are going to do right now. Close your *ClassName.java* file and create a new one. Let's just call this *main.java*. A pretty bad name in my opinion, but it's what I went with so I'm going to stick with it.

In our *main.java* class, we're just going to want to create the class and standard *main()* method. The *public static void main(String[] args) main()* method. This is why *main.java* is a bad name!

You should have something like this:

```
class main {

    public static void main(String[] args) {

    }
}
```

Now make the following additions:

```
class main {

    public static void main(String[] args) {
        ClassName c1 = new ClassName();
        ClassName c2 = new ClassName(10,10);

        System.out.println("c1 var1 = " +
                                    c1.getVar1());
        System.out.println("c1 var2 = " +
                                    c1.getVar2());
        System.out.println("c2 var1 = " +
                                    c2.getVar1());
        System.out.println("c2 var2 = " +
                                    c2.getVar2());

        c1.setVar1(200);
        c2.setVar1(600);
```

```
        System.out.println("c1 var1 = " +
                                        c1.getVar1());
        System.out.println("c2 var1 = " +
                                        c2.getVar1());

    }
}
```

As you can see there are quite a few new lines, most of them just output some data though so get your copy & paste on! Go ahead and compile this *main.java* file, the compiler will also automatically compile *ClassName.java* as long as it is in the same directory. Then run *main.java*.

The first two new lines:

```
ClassName c1 = new ClassName();
ClassName c2 = new ClassName(10,10);
```

This is the declaration and instantiation of our *ClassName* object. Look familiar? It's essentially just another variable declaration but instead of a primitive data type, our type is the name of our class. The *new* keyword tells Java to allocate enough memory on the heap for the class we are instantiating. Following that, we have what appears to be a function call. That's because it is. We're calling the constructor method within the class we're instantiating to create a new instance of it. You'll see the first line calls the constructor with no parameters and the second calls the constructor with parameters. We now have 2 instances of our *ClassName* class called *c1* and *c2*. These are objects.

Dot Notation

In order to access methods within an object, we use dot notation. Sometimes referred to as the dot operator. We can see this in use in every *System.out.println()* statement in the above code. You'll see

```
c1.getVar1()
```
or

```
c2.getVar1()
```
etc.

This tells Java to look inside object *c1,* which is an instance of our class *ClassName,* and execute the *getVar1()* method which returns the value of the *integer* variable *var1.* If this method was *private* or it didn't exist, we'd encounter an exception, more on that later. It's not just methods that can be accessed this way, however. Variables can be too, if they exhibit the required access modifiers. If we change *var1* to *public,* we would then be able to simply type

```
c1.var1
```
to both get and set the value of the variable, just like any other variable.

Nested classes

I just wanted to briefly touch on nested classes although it is somewhat beyond the intended scope of this book. But I feel you should be made aware of them so you can further research them if there comes a time where you feel they'd benefit your work.

Java allows you to create classes within classes. These are referred to as nested classes. A nested class may be one of two types, either a static nested class or a non-static nested class, the latter is referred to simply as an inner class.

When you define an inner class, it has access to all member variables and methods of the containing class, even if they are *private*. This is one of the reasons that nested classes are used, to increase encapsulation in this way. Nesting small classes within top-level classes enables the inner class code to be located closer to where it is used which may aid development. Inner classes behave similarly to other member variables within the top-level, or outer, class. Static nested classes do not. They are equivalent to having a top-level class nested within another top-level class.

```
class outerClass {
    class innerClass {
    }
}
```

This is essentially how a nested class would look. If you require more information regarding nested classes, please refer to the online Java documentation.

1. Classes generally represent objects
2. You should give all member variables and functions an access modifier
3. You don't need to define a class constructor but it is a good idea to do so
4. Constructors can be overloaded
5. When you instantiate a class you are creating an instance of it, a copy of it
6. Use dot notation (the dot operator) to access member variables and methods
7. The *this* keyword refers to the class of which the code is contained within
8. Make use of *getter* and *setter* methods

Exercises

Create a class that can represents a provided temperature in both Celsius and Fahrenheit, similar to the program we wrote in Chapter 8. The class constructor should take the unit type (i.e. Celsius or Fahrenheit) and a temperature value. It should then convert the given value to the alternative unit type and store both values. There should be a *getter* and *setter* method for each value. The *setter* methods should also take the liberty of converting the temperature to the other format by means of some private methods, *toCelsius()* and *toFahrenheit()* from Chapter 8 would be useful here. Finally, you should create a separate class to contain the main entry point to your program and then create and instantiate your temperature object, providing it with the value 30 Celsius. You should then access your *getter* methods for both Celsius and Fahrenheit and output the result. Your result should be 30 and 86 respectively. Test your *setter* method for Celsius and then display your updated results and then test your *setter* method for Fahrenheit and display your updated results again. Once we've looked into error handling, we will begin making use of the *Scanner* class, demonstrated in Chapter 8, more. That'll conclude the exercise for Chapter 12. If you fancy an extra challenge, use the *Scanner* class to take user input and allow the user to choose which temperature unit they want to convert from and to and the value of that temperature. I won't be including this extension in the solutions at the back of the book, though, because I demonstrate this functionality in Chapter 8 and don't fancy repeating myself just yet!

Chapter 13: Error Handling

Error handling is essential to any robust program. If your program rolls over and dies (aka becomes unresponsive then terminates or just terminates) then it's not a very good program, let's be honest.

Non-specific to Java, there are three types of error that one encounters. You have compile errors which prevent the program from being compiled - things like trying to use a variable that doesn't exist, forgetting to end a line with a semi-colon or forgetting a closing curly brace somewhere. These are the best errors. The compiler complains and won't compile your program so the problem will never make it to a final product. The compiler also gives you a good indication (usually) of what the problem is so it's not too difficult to fix (usually).

You then have runtime errors which generally cause your program to crash and burn (terminate prematurely). These can be caused by trying to access elements in an array with an index that is larger than the number of elements or running out of memory, for example. Runtime errors can generally be anticipated and handled within your code to minimize their chance of occurrence but not every situation can be accounted for.

Finally, my least favourite type of error, the logic error. It isn't an error as such but more of a problem with the logic of your program. The compiler won't point it out and it won't cause a runtime error, you'll just get different outcomes than you'd expect. For example, 1+1 always equals 2 but a logic error might result in 1+1 being equal to 7. That's just a vague example, though. Anything that results in the incorrect functionality of your program, whether data output or clicking a button and ending up on the wrong screen, can be classified as a logic error. Some programmers do tend to refer only to the logic of code that results in output when referring to logic errors though so bear this in mind.

Dealing with Compiler Errors

Compiler errors are any error that prevents your program from compiling. There are also *checked exceptions* which will prevent Java programs from compiling but these are discussed below. This section deals exclusively with non-exception errors. For example, let's say you forget to use a closing curly brace in your code somewhere. You'll most likely get the message:

```
error: reached end of file while parsing
```

This isn't very helpful. It simply says that the compiler has reached the end of the file unexpectedly, it's due to parse some more stuff before finishing. This is a good indicator that you've missed a closing curly brace somewhere. It doesn't really indicate where, though, so a good starting point is anywhere you've made recent changes. If you can't find anything there, you have a meticulous task of locating the issue on your hands, best of luck!

Other compiler errors in Java include forgetting to close a String:

```
x: error: unclosed string literal
```

x will represent the line number where your unclosed string literal may be found, or perhaps a line or two before. A nice easy to find error.

```
x: error: ';' expected
```

Again, x will represent the line number where your problem lies, this time a missing semi-colon. You may also see this error if you try to name variables with a keyword, for example.

```
x: error: cannot find symbol
    someSymbol()
    ^
```

This error means that you are trying to use a method that does not exist or you have mistyped the name of. The same error message will apply to variables that do not exist or you have mistyped the name of. The line number of the source of the error is indicated.

106

```
x: error: illegal start of expression
```
You'll probably come across this compiler error if you mistype *for()* when creating a *for* loop, forget to include a condition in an *if* statement or perhaps some other scenarios. A line number will be provided which is generally a pretty good indicator in locating the problem.

```
x: error: 'else' without 'if'
```
A pretty self explanatory error, trying to use *else* without an *if* clause.

The best way to resolve multiple compiler errors is to start from the very first one. Every time you make a change to your code, compile it again. If you're on the right track, the number of errors should gradually reduce. You should always try and resolve the first error first because it may be the cause of any other error that is occurring.

Exceptions

Java utilises *exceptions* to handle errors. This refers to any exceptional event which, during the execution of a program, disrupts the normal flow of a program's instructions. The runtime errors described previous are dealt with in this section. There are *three* kinds of exception in Java:- *Checked exceptions, errors* and *runtime exceptions*. When exceptions occur, they are said to be *thrown*. An object is created to represent an exception and something has to catch it. When any exception is thrown, the runtime system attempts to find something to handle it, this is known as an exception handler. An exception can either be caught at the point of occurrence in which the code is contained within a *try-catch* block, an exception handler, **or** the method that contains the code can *throw* the exception which then passes it up the call stack until an exception handler is found. If no exception handler is found then the runtime system and program will terminate. This is usually the case for *errors* and *runtime exceptions*, you will see why in the next section.

Checked Exceptions and the *catch or specify requirement*

Checked exceptions are those that a well-written program should be able to recover from. For example, attempting to open a file that does not exist would produce a checked exception. The program should cater for this scenario by catching the exception, notifying the user and perhaps allowing them to correct their mistake and continue with the program. Checked exceptions are subject to what Java refers to as the *catch or specify requirement*. This requirement means that code that may throw certain types of exception must be enclosed in either a *try-catch* block or within a method that *throws* the exception. Neither *errors* or *runtime exceptions* are subject to this requirement.

Unchecked Exceptions

The other two types of exception are collectively referred to as unchecked exceptions because they are not required to honour the *catch or specify requirement* which means code that may produce such errors will compile whether or not it is contained within a *try-catch* block or method which *throws* an exception.

The *error* exception is a type of exception that is external to the program and the program may not be able to anticipate such errors or recover from them. For example, attempting to open a file that is corrupt would result in an *error* because the file exists but it cannot be opened. You may catch this type of exception in order to handle it but it is not a requirement. Of course, it would be sensible to handle such possibilities appropriately because simply letting your program crash is not good form and this would be the outcome of not handling *error* exceptions. As mentioned, though, not all *errors* can be anticipated so try not to worry too much about every unknown eventuality; if an unhandled *error* exception is thrown then your program will terminate and print a stack trace to help you debug and resolve the cause.

The *runtime exception* is the third type of exception. Unlike errors, *runtime exceptions* are exceptions that are internal to the program but are unlikely to be anticipated and/or recovered from. A typical example of this would be trying to access a variable or array that is yet to be initialized. This will create a NullPointerException. Again, you may choose to catch these errors or just let them play out which will result in program termination and a printout of a stack trace. Alternatively, and more sensibly, you can strive to eliminate these exceptions all together by rectifying the problems that cause them.

Okay, enough rambling. That's the "under the hood" version, let's take a look at how to actually handle some exceptions!

Exception Handlers

Exception handlers are simply *try-catch* blocks which I've used several times in the previous chapters already. The *try-catch* block is rarely called an exception handler but that's what it is. So, let's take a closer look at *try-catch*.

First of all, here's the kind of message you can expect the compiler to spit out if you try to use code that *may throw* a *checked* exception:

```
C:\Windows\system32\cmd.exe

d:\Desktop\java>javac Test.java
Test.java:8: error: unreported exception FileNotFoundException; must be caught o
r declared to be thrown
        file_in = new FileInputStream("C:/some_file.txt");
                  ^
1 error

d:\Desktop\java>
```

The FileNotFoundException is a checked exception and the code will not compile without handling it correctly. You'll see that the message is:

```
Test.java:8: error: unreported exception
FileNotFoundException; must be caught or declared to be
thrown
```

this is our problem. The next line shows us where the problem arises:

```
        file_in = new FileInputStream("C:/some_file.txt");
                  ^
1 error
```

The "1 error" text indicates how many errors the compiler has found, the caret (^) shows where our problem is coming from. It's pointing at "*new*

FileInputStream(..." which gives us a good indication that this line is causing our error. To fix this, we need to handle the checked exception and this can be achieved with a *try-catch* block.

A *try-catch* block looks like this:

```
try {
    //do something
} catch(Exception e) {
    //handle exception
}
```

We replace "//do something" with our code that throws a checked exception and "//handle exception" with some code that should execute if the exception is thrown. We also replace the word *Exception* with the specific exception we are targeting, in this case that's a FileNotFoundException!

Following is the erroneous code and then the correct code respectively.

```
import java.io.*;

class Test {

    public static void main(String[] args) {

        FileInputStream file_in = null;
        file_in = new FileInputStream("C:/some_file.txt");

    } //end main()
}
```

Go ahead and compile this code to get a grasp on what's going on.

```
import java.io.*;

class Test {

    public static void main(String[] args) {

        FileInputStream file_in = null;

        try {
```

```
            file_in = new
FileInputStream("C:/some_file.txt");
    } catch(FileNotFoundException e) {
            e.printStackTrace();
    }

  } //end main()

}
```

The second code sample will compile without error. It doesn't do much, though, if you run it you'll see the stack trace which is basically a print out of the methods currently in the call stack leading back to the source of the error. Unless, of course, *C:/some_file.txt* exists on your system!

That's not a particularly helpful message to the user, though, so go ahead and change

```
e.printStackTrace();
```
to

```
System.out.println( e.getMessage() );
```

and compare the outputs.

In this particular example, you would probably opt to use the *getMessage()* method and then ask the user to provide a new file path to an existing file in order to allow the continuation of the program.

So, how do we know which exceptions may be thrown? Well, you could just attempt to compile your code and deal with each of the exceptions as and when they pop up or you could take a look at the Java documentation which is what you'd be expected to do whenever using new Java methods and/or objects that are part of Java which you have not used before.

That's how to handle checked exceptions but what about unchecked exceptions? What if we wanted to convert user input to a number, which we do in a previous chapter, but the user input is not numeric. Compile the following code and note that no error occurs.

```
class NotNumeric {

    public static void main(String[] args) {

        String str = "a";

        Integer.parseInt(str);
```

```
    } //end main()

}
```

Then run the code and observe the exception!

```
C:\Windows\system32\cmd.exe                                   _  □  ×

d:\Desktop\java>java NotNumeric
java.lang.NumberFormatException: For input string: "a"
        at java.lang.NumberFormatException.forInputString(Unknown Source)
        at java.lang.Integer.parseInt(Unknown Source)
        at java.lang.Integer.parseInt(Unknown Source)
        at NotNumeric.main(NotNumeric.java:7)

d:\Desktop\java>
```

This exception is thrown by the method *Integer.parseInt()* on line 7 of *NotNumeric.java*. So let's take a look at line 7:

```
Integer.parseInt(a);
```

All we're doing is passing a variable to the *parseInt()* method of *Integer* which takes a string and converts it to an integer, there's nothing wrong here. So our next stop is to take a look at the variable we are passing to this method which is on line 5.

```
String str = "a";
```

Here's our problem. "a" is not an integer. Go ahead and change the value of *str* to an integer string like so:

```
String str = "100";
```

and then compile and run the code again. Notice that nothing actually happens but no exception is thrown either, the code executes fully without interruption. That's not an ideal solution, though. All we did was fix the *cause* of this instance of the error. We didn't implement any solution to handle future errors. Change your code to match the code below to see a more permanent fix:

This page intentionally blank

```
class NotNumeric {

    public static void main(String[] args) {

      String str = "a";

      try {
            Integer.parseInt(str);
      } catch(NumberFormatException e) {
            System.out.println( "\"" + str + "\" is not an
                                          integer" );

      }

    } //end main()

}
```

Here we've placed the line that *may* throw an exception within a *try-catch* block in order to handle any *NumberFormatException* exceptions that it may throw. This way, no matter what value we pass to the *parseInt()* method, if it's not an integer the exception will be caught and the user informed.

This is a *runtime exception.* The second type of exception, the *error* exception, won't be demonstrated here because you may handle them in the same manner as both *checked* and *runtime exception* exceptions.

Throwing Exceptions

Now we've caught some exceptions, what about throwing them? Moreover, what does that mean?!

All the exceptions we catch are thrown. You can't catch something if it's not thrown, right? Right. Instead of catching an exception when it's thrown, we can throw it further. If you have a method, *methodOne()* for simplicity, which has some code that causes an exception, and you don't want *methodOne()* to handle that exception, you can throw the exception up the call stack to the point where the *methodOne()* method is called instead.

Let's see that in action so it's a little easier to understand.

```java
class NotNumeric {

    public static void main(String[] args) {

        String str = "a";

        methodOne(str);

    } //end main()

    static void methodOne(String s) throws
                            NumberFormatException {
        Integer.parseInt(s);
    }
}
```

Look at the declaration of the *methodOne()* method. There are the words "throws NumberFormatException". What this means is that any *NumberFormatException* that is thrown within the method is thrown further up to where the method is called. If you compile and run this code, you'll get the following stack trace:

```
C:\Windows\system32\cmd.exe

d:\Desktop\java>java NotNumeric
Exception in thread "main" java.lang.NumberFormatException: For input string: "a
"
        at java.lang.NumberFormatException.forInputString(Unknown Source)
        at java.lang.Integer.parseInt(Unknown Source)
        at java.lang.Integer.parseInt(Unknown Source)
        at NotNumeric.methodOne(NotNumeric.java:12)
        at NotNumeric.main(NotNumeric.java:7)

d:\Desktop\java>
```

Again, at the bottom of the trace, we see that *NotNumeric.java:7* is displayed which means a problem is starting on line 7 of *NotNumeric.java*. If we go to this line, there's a call to *methodOne()*. The next line up in the stack trace also shows this. It points us to line 12 of *NotNumeric.java*. Of course, line 12 is just a call to *Integer.parseInt()* and so we should look at the variable that is passed to this method. We then see that the variable passed to *parseInt()* is the variable passed to *methodOne()* so we have to go back to line 7 and see what the variable is. We can then see that variable *str* is passed to *methodOne()* and when looking at the variable, it's clear that it is not an integer. In a very similar fashion to the *runtime exception* that we previously looked at, we need to use a *try-catch* block here. This time, though, the *try-catch* block is not used at the point where the exception is initially thrown (*Integer.parseInt()*) but instead it is used to encapsulate the call to *methodOne()*. So we end up with the following code:

```
class NotNumeric {

    public static void main(String[] args) {

        String str = "a";

        try {
            methodOne(str);

        } catch(NumberFormatException e) {
```

```
            System.out.println( "\"" + str + "\" is not an
integer" );
        }

    } //end main()

    static void methodOne(String s) throws
                           NumberFormatException {
        Integer.parseInt(s);
    }
}
```

What this means is that if the code in *methodOne()* happens to throw a *NumberFormatException* exception, it'll be thrown further to the point that *methodOne()* was called and then handled there instead. The *main()* method can also throw exceptions in this way, but this would result in the program terminating instead of handling the exception. See the following code to demonstrate:

```
class NotNumeric {

    public static void main(String[] args) throws
                            NumberFormatException {

        String str = "a";

        methodOne(str);

    } //end main()

    static void methodOne(String s) throws
                            NumberFormatException {
        Integer.parseInt(s);
    }
}
```

This is essentially the same as not handling the exception at all, however.

Custom Exceptions and Throwing New Exceptions

Although beyond the scope of this book, it's prudent to note that you can also create custom exceptions to better suit your needs. This is more for larger scale projects where the default Java exceptions are too vague or different from the type of exception you wish to throw.

The previous section talks of throwing exceptions further up the stack. These exceptions are initially thrown at some point, though. Think of this as the first throw. This is achieved by using the *throw* keyword. Notice the lack of an **s**. This is called throwing a *new* exception.

Study, copy, compile and execute the following code:

```java
class ManualThrow {

    public static void main(String[] args) {

        try {
                throw new Exception("Test exception");
        }
        catch (Exception e) {
System.out.println(e.getMessage());}

    } //end main()
}
```

This code creates a new Exception object with a custom message and then throws it, catches it and then shows the message to the user. This is how the initial throw of an exception is done.

1. Check the documentation if you're not sure what type of exceptions may be thrown. This way you can be sure you can catch unchecked exceptions too, if necessary
2. Use *try-catch* blocks whenever a piece of code may throw an exception, even if it is an unchecked exception
3. Resolve compiler errors sequentially, starting at the beginning and recompiling after each error is resolved
4. Use the information the compiler or stack trace gives you to debug your program and resolve exceptions

Chapter 14: Inheritance and Polymorphism

Inheritance is a core feature of Object Oriented Programming. Think back to classes. Each class represents an object. Inheritance allows us to create a *parent class* which can pass on all methods and variables to *child classes*, similar to how a human parent would pass on DNA to their child. It is said that the *child class* **inherits** its *parent's* members. Java tends to use the terms *super class* and *subclass* as opposed to *parent class* and *child class* respectively. I will probably use them interchangeably.

Why have Inheritance

Some people find it somewhat challenging to wrap their head around inheritance so I'm going to do away with the long winded explanations and just dive straight into it! Imagine we have a game, this is a typical example of inheritance. We won't be making a game, by the way, this is just a demonstration of inheritance! Our game has **animals**. We have **dogs, cats, dinosaurs, lions** and **humans**. I mean calling a person an animal isn't the nicest thing in the world but hey, humans do have those animalistic tendencies, right?

All the words in bold will be classes. Let's think for a moment what kind of data our dogs, cats, dinosaurs, lions and humans have in common:

1. legs
2. eyes
3. fur
4. color

Our animals will also have a movement speed and, if we want to be super precise, location coordinates. I'm sure there's plenty else we could add but this shall suffice for our purpose. Think back to Chapter 12 regarding classes. If you didn't read this chapter, I'm going to be talking about *getters* and *setters*. So, for the 6 points above (4 + movement speed and location), we'll need a *getter* method. We'll only need a *setter* method for the location because the other stuff won't be changing after it's initially set.

Following are five pages of code, please skip to the last one.

Dog.java

```java
class Dog {

    private int numOfLegs = 0;
    private String eyeColor = "";
    private boolean hasFur = false;
    private String bodyColor = "";
    private int posX = 0;
    private int posY = 0;

    public Dog(int numOfLegs, String eyeColor, boolean
                         hasFur, String bodyColor) {
        this.numOfLegs = numOfLegs;
        this.eyeColor = eyeColor;
        this.hasFur = hasFur;
        this.bodyColor = bodyColor;
    }

    public int getNumOfLegs() {
        return numOfLegs;
    }

    public String getEyeColor() {
        return eyeColor;
    }

    public boolean getHasFur() {
        return hasFur;
    }

    public String getBodyColor() {
        return bodyColor;
    }

    public int getPosX() {
        return posX;
    }

    public int getPosY() {
        return posY;
    }
```

```java
    public void setPos(int x, int y) {
        posX = x;
        posY = y;
    }
}
```

Cat.java

```java
class Cat {

    private int numOfLegs = 0;
    private String eyeColor = "";
    private boolean hasFur = false;
    private String bodyColor = "";
    private int posX = 0;
    private int posY = 0;

    public Cat(int numOfLegs, String eyeColor, boolean
                              hasFur, String bodyColor) {
        this.numOfLegs = numOfLegs;
        this.eyeColor = eyeColor;
        this.hasFur = hasFur;
        this.bodyColor = bodyColor;
    }

    public int getNumOfLegs() {
        return numOfLegs;
    }

    public String getEyeColor() {
        return eyeColor;
    }

    public boolean getHasFur() {
        return hasFur;
    }

    public String getBodyColor() {
        return bodyColor;
    }

    public int getPosX() {
        return posX;
    }

    public int getPosY() {
        return posY;
    }

    public void setPos(int x, int y) {
```

```
        posX = x;
        posY = y;
    }
}
```

Dinosaur.java

```java
class Dinosaur {

    private int numOfLegs = 0;
    private String eyeColor = "";
    private boolean hasFur = false;
    private String bodyColor = "";
    private int posX = 0;
    private int posY = 0;

    public Dinosaur(int numOfLegs, String eyeColor,
                boolean hasFur, String bodyColor) {
        this.numOfLegs = numOfLegs;
        this.eyeColor = eyeColor;
        this.hasFur = hasFur;
        this.bodyColor = bodyColor;
    }

    public int getNumOfLegs() {
        return numOfLegs;
    }

    public String getEyeColor() {
        return eyeColor;
    }

    public boolean getHasFur() {
        return hasFur;
    }

    public String getBodyColor() {
        return bodyColor;
    }

    public int getPosX() {
        return posX;
    }

    public int getPosY() {
        return posY;
    }

    public void setPos(int x, int y) {
```

```
        posX = x;
        posY = y;
    }
}
```

Lion.java

```java
class Lion {

    private int numOfLegs = 0;
    private String eyeColor = "";
    private boolean hasFur = false;
    private String bodyColor = "";
    private int posX = 0;
    private int posY = 0;

    public Lion(int numOfLegs, String eyeColor, boolean
                         hasFur, String bodyColor) {
        this.numOfLegs = numOfLegs;
        this.eyeColor = eyeColor;
        this.hasFur = hasFur;
        this.bodyColor = bodyColor;
    }

    public int getNumOfLegs() {
        return numOfLegs;
    }

    public String getEyeColor() {
        return eyeColor;
    }

    public boolean getHasFur() {
        return hasFur;
    }

    public String getBodyColor() {
        return bodyColor;
    }

    public int getPosX() {
        return posX;
    }

    public int getPosY() {
        return posY;
    }

    public void setPos(int x, int y) {
```

```
        posX = x;
        posY = y;
    }
}
```

Human.java

```java
class Human {

    private int numOfLegs = 0;
    private String eyeColor = "";
    private boolean hasFur = false;
    private String bodyColor = "";
    private int posX = 0;
    private int posY = 0;

    public Human(int numOfLegs, String eyeColor, boolean
                            hasFur, String bodyColor) {
        this.numOfLegs = numOfLegs;
        this.eyeColor = eyeColor;
        this.hasFur = hasFur;
        this.bodyColor = bodyColor;
    }

    public int getNumOfLegs() {
        return numOfLegs;
    }

    public String getEyeColor() {
        return eyeColor;
    }

    public boolean getHasFur() {
        return hasFur;
    }

    public String getBodyColor() {
        return bodyColor;
    }

    public int getPosX() {
        return posX;
    }

    public int getPosY() {
        return posY;
    }

    public void setPos(int x, int y) {
```

```
        posX = x;
        posY = y;
    }
}
```

So that's pretty silly, isn't it? Each class represents an animal but they all contain the same member variables and methods. So much repetition! This is where inheritance comes in. Now we need our **Animal** class:

With Inheritance

Animal.java

```
class Animal {
    private int numOfLegs = 0;
    private String eyeColor = "";
    private boolean hasFur = false;
    private String bodyColor = "";
    private int posX = 0;
    private int posY = 0;
    private int speed = 0;

    public Animal(int numOfLegs, String eyeColor,
            boolean hasFur, String bodyColor, int speed) {
        this.numOfLegs = numOfLegs;
        this.eyeColor = eyeColor;
        this.hasFur = hasFur;
        this.bodyColor = bodyColor;
        this.speed = speed;
    }
    public int getNumOfLegs() {
        return numOfLegs;
    }
    public String getEyeColor() {
        return eyeColor;
    }
    public boolean getHasFur() {
        return hasFur;
    }
    public String getBodyColor() {
        return bodyColor;
    }
    public int getPosX() {
        return posX;
    }
    public int getPosY() {
        return posY;
    }
```

```java
    public int getSpeed() {
        return speed;
    }
    public void setPos(int x, int y) {
        posX = x;
        posY = y;
    }
}
```

Now we have a *parent class*, we can pass on its member variables and methods to our animal classes. To achieve this, we use the ***extends*** keyword. Now, our 5 animal classes look like this instead:

dogs, cats, dinosaurs, lions and **humans**

```
class Dog extends Animal {
    public Dog(int numOfLegs, String eyeColor, boolean
            hasFur, String bodyColor, int speed) {
        super(numOfLegs, eyeColor, hasFur, bodyColor,
                                            speed);
    }
}


class Cat extends Animal {
    public Cat(int numOfLegs, String eyeColor, boolean
            hasFur, String bodyColor, int speed) {
        super(numOfLegs, eyeColor, hasFur, bodyColor,
                                            speed);
    }
}


class Dinosaur extends Animal {
    public Dinosaur(int numOfLegs, String eyeColor,
        boolean hasFur, String bodyColor, int speed) {
        super(numOfLegs, eyeColor, hasFur, bodyColor,
                                            speed);
    }
}


class Lion extends Animal {
    public Lion(int numOfLegs, String eyeColor, boolean
            hasFur, String bodyColor, int speed) {
        super(numOfLegs, eyeColor, hasFur, bodyColor,
                                            speed);
    }
}
```

```
class Human extends Animal {
    public Human(int numOfLegs, String eyeColor, boolean
            hasFur, String bodyColor, int speed) {
        super(numOfLegs, eyeColor, hasFur, bodyColor,
                                          speed);
    }
}
```

Look how much we have shortened our code we have by using inheritance. All of our animal classes, **Dog, Cat, Lion, Dinosaur** and **Human** look almost empty! Of course, they're not. They *inherit* all the variables and methods from **Animal.java**. Take note of the keyword *extends* at the start of the class:

```
class Dog extends Animal {
```

The next line we need to observe is this:

```
super(numOfLegs, eyeColor, hasFur, bodyColor, speed);
```

The *super()* keyword is used to access a *parent class* constructor. That is what is happening here. We take the parameters passed to our *child class constructor* and call the constructor of our *parent class* with those parameters, using the *super()* keyword. The *super()* keyword takes as many parameters as the *parent class* that it refers to.

Now we need to test our classes. To do this, we simply create another test class with a *main()* method and create an instance of one of our animals and access the *getter()* methods like so:

```
class inheritanceTest {
    public static void main(String[] args) {
        Dog dog = new Dog(4, "blue", true, "brown",
                                                1);

        System.out.println("# legs: " +
                                dog.getNumOfLegs() );
        System.out.println("Eye color: " +
                                dog.getEyeColor() );
        System.out.println("Has fur?: " +
                                dog.getHasFur() );
        System.out.println("Color: " +
                                dog.getBodyColor() );
        System.out.println("Speed: " + dog.getSpeed()
                                                );
    }
}
```

We can adjust this class to test the other animal classes too by just changing the variable type from *Dog* to one of our other animal classes. I haven't changed the variable name, just the type, so we can save time for testing purposes:

```
class inheritanceTest {
    public static void main(String[] args) {

        Cat dog = new Cat(4, "blue", true, "brown",
                                                1);

        System.out.println("# legs: " +
                                    dog.getNumOfLegs() );
        System.out.println("Eye color: " +
                                    dog.getEyeColor() );
        System.out.println("Has fur?: " +
                                    dog.getHasFur() );
        System.out.println("Color: " +
                                    dog.getBodyColor() );
        System.out.println("Speed: " + dog.getSpeed()
                                                );
    }
}
```

As you can see from this example, inheritance is an incredibly powerful technique for reusability and efficiency. You should turn to inheritance whenever you find yourself wanting to create a new class whereby another class exists with some of the code you want to use in your new class. If you plan your projects carefully, you should be able to anticipate the best opportunities to use inheritance without inheriting too much unused code.

Polymorphism

Polymorphism, some find, is a rather complex topic to understand and explain so I will discuss the previous part of this chapter some more in order to portray the concept. Polymorphism means to take on many different forms (poly = many, morph = form, shape). In relation to programming, it simply means the overloading or overriding of methods and the declaration of objects. Inheritance and polymorphism go hand-in-hand, there would be no polymorphism without Inheritance. Let's take our *inheritanceTest* class from previous and change the following line:

```
Cat dog = new Cat(4, "blue", true, "brown", 1);
```
to

```
Animal dog = new Cat(4, "blue", true, "brown", 1);
```

This will not affect how the code functions because *Cat* is indeed an Animal and our class hierarchy represents this. The *Cat* class inherits the *Animal* class and is therefore both an *Animal* class **and** a *Cat* class. This is just a part of the concept of polymorphism, though. As I previously mentioned, method overloading is also a form of polymorphism. Method overloading is discussed in Chapter 7 on functions so please review the chapter if you need a refresher on function overloading. As for how it relates to polymorphism - well, a function does something, an overloaded function (should) do the same thing but with a different signature. i.e. an overloaded function will take different parameters. This alteration that allows the creation of an overloaded method is in itself polymorphism within Java.

Another part of polymorphism in Java is method overriding. This means that we have a parent class with a particular method and we want our child class to have the same method but with a slightly different process. For example, if we take a look at our *Animal.java* class above and note the method *getEyeColor()*, then we have our *Dog.java* class which inherits this method, we can give *Dog.java* its own *getEyeColor()* method which would override the method that is written in *Animal.java*. To do this, we would simply write a *getEyeColor()* method within our *Dog.java* class and have it perform whatever functionality is desired. Change *Dog.java* to look like this and see the effect:

```
class Dog extends Animal {
    public Dog(int numOfLegs, String eyeColor, boolean
            hasFur, String bodyColor, int speed) {
        super(numOfLegs, eyeColor, hasFur, bodyColor,
                                                speed);
    }

    public String getEyeColor() {
        return "always brown";
    }
}
```

Now, whenever we create an instance of *Dog.java* and call *getEyeColor()* the value "always brown" will be returned despite the value actually passed on instantiation.

Polymorphism isn't really one particular thing that you learn, like an *if-statement* or *function* but instead is a concept that reflects the principles of something taking on one or more forms. So remember, if you're using overloaded or overridden functions then you're making use of polymorphism.

Key Points

1. Inheritance in the context of object oriented programming means to inherit the methods and variables from a parent class
2. You should use inheritance whenever you need to reuse the code contained within a class in another class
3. classes can only inherit from one parent class, I forgot to mention this before so take note!
4. Polymorphism isn't a particular technique or syntax that you learn but instead is a concept which includes method overloading and method overriding

Exercises

There's just one exercise for this chapter as there will be another *Intermission* chapter in the not so distant future and I don't want you to be spending too much time with inheritance, one you understand it you understand it! So, let's say we have a banking system with three types of account:

1. Personal
2. Business (Small Business)
3. Commercial (Huge Business)

Each of these accounts have to store the following common information:

1. Account Number
2. Account Holder
3. Account Balance
4. Transaction History (Use an ArrayList)
5. Transaction fee (%) for withdrawals

Remember, classes represent (usually tangible) objects so each account type should be represented by on object of its own.

In addition to this common information, the business and commercial accounts should also store the business type that the business represents (e.g. motor industry, food industry, entertainment, computing etc).

Your objective is to create some classes that represent this system by using inheritance. Create a *BankingSystem* class to contain the *main()* entry point of your program and create an account of each type with some appropriate data. You should also make amendments to the data too and, if a change to the account balance is made, add a transaction entry. You will need a method for performing transactions.

Chapter 15: Interfaces

Interfaces are so named based on the idea that methods within a class are the interface in which objects can be interacted with from the outside world. In Java, an interface is similar to a class in that they can declare methods and variables, with one key difference. An interface method **cannot have a body. Variables declared within an *interface* are *final* meaning that they cannot be changed.** When you declare a method within an interface, you simply write out the method signature and then whack a semi-colon on the end. There's no opening and closing curly brace and no code in between.

So, what does an interface look like? A class, of course! The only difference is we replace the word *class* with *interface*. The filename will still have to match the interface name, like a class name must match the filename.

```
interface NewInterface {

    public void someMethod();
}
```

There we go, that's the essence of an interface. To make use of an interface, we use the *implements* keyword. Like so:

```
class NewClass implements NewInterface {

}
```

Go ahead and create these two files and compile *NewClass.java* and see what happens.

The thing you'll immediately notice is a compiler error telling you that NewClass is not abstract and does not override abstract method *someMethod()* in *NewInterface*. This is saying that your *NewClass* class must have a method called *someMethod()*. That's the beauty of interfaces. They can define methods that must be implemented by any class that implements the interface, otherwise the class will not compile. On top of this, a class an implement as many interfaces as you want. You can only *inherit* from **one** class but you can use many interfaces. Interfaces are implemented after you inherit from a class so your class, if inheriting from a parent class and implementing interfaces, will always look like this:

```
class NewClass extends SomeParent implements
NewInterface1, NewInterface2
```
extends first and then *implements*.

Let's take a look at a potential use for the *interface*:

```
interface Car {

    int topSpeed = 100;

    public double getFuelLevel();

    public int getTopSpeed();

    public void toggleEngine();

}
```

This is just a simple *interface* intended to represent a car. All modern cars show the current fuel level, have a top speed and an engine which can start (we hope!). We also provide a top speed of 100, we can decide a unit for this value later. This value cannot change as members in an *interface* are *final*. Anything implementing our *interface* would have to honour the requirement that our three methods **must** be implemented.

```java
class FourByFourCar implements Car {

    private boolean engineStarted = false;
    private double fuelLevel = 100;

    public double getFuelLevel() {
        return fuelLevel;
    }

    public int getTopSpeed() {
        return topSpeed;
    }

    public void toggleEngine() {
        engineStarted = !engineStarted;
    }

    public String getEngineState() {
        return (engineStarted) ? "on" : "off";
    }

    public static void main(String[] args) {

        FourByFourCar f = new FourByFourCar();

        System.out.println("Fuel: " + f.getFuelLevel()
+ "%");
        System.out.println("Top Speed: " +
                        f.getTopSpeed() + "mph");
        System.out.println("Engine is " +
                            f.getEngineState());
        f.toggleEngine();
        System.out.println("Engine is " +
                            f.getEngineState());

    }
}
```

Our *FourByFourCar* class represents a 4x4, of course, but it implements the *Car interface* so it must implement the *getTopSpeed(), toggleEngine()* and *getFuelLevel()* methods in order to compile successfully. We create a *boolean* to represent whether or not the engine is running and a *double* to store the fuel level as a percentage and then implement the required methods which return the top speed, defined and declared within the *interface* itself, return the fuel level and toggle the engine state.

Of course, we could just write our *FourByFourCar* class without the *Car interface* and implement the methods anyway but the *interface* serves as a blueprint that must be followed. This blueprint, however, doesn't define *how* something is done, just that *it has to be done*.

Key Points

1. An interface can declare methods and variables but the variables are *final* and the methods do not have a body, just a signature
2. A class can implement as many interfaces as you want
3. the *implements* keyword must be used after the *extends* keyword if you are using both

Chapter 16: Putting it all together

In this chapter we're going to put everything we've learnt together and create a fully functional command-line program to conclude the book. We'll be using pretty much everything discussed throughout the book with the exception of *interfaces*.

Packages

Before we start, we need a crash course on packages because we're going to have several classes and it's not very professional to have an unpackaged project with multiple classes. The best way to describe a package is to compare it to a folder / directory on your system; If we had a package called *ThePackage*, for example, we would have a directory called *ThePackage* and all classes will be contained within this folder. That's pretty much what we've done, right? Yes... BUT we must also declare the files to be a part of the package, too. To do this, we use the *package* keyword which is to be included at the start of any Java file that is within a package.

```
package ThePackage;
```

This is the line we would put at the very beginning of our classes within the package. Generally speaking, you don't need to worry about the structure of packages when using an Integrated Development Environment (IDE) because the environment takes care of all that for you but for the next section of this chapter, we will be creating *one* package for our project. Now that you're armed with that knowledge, let's continue!

A University System

What exactly will we be making? Let's imagine a university scenario. We need a system to represent the university. We could create this entire system but we don't want to do that, it'd be a ridiculously big project, a bit beyond what I have in mind. But a university, of course, has many departments. Naturally, we're going to focus on the Computing Department, since that would be most fitting. We shall create a system that represents a Computing Department at some university.

Let's consider what we will want our system to do, what it will need. Bear in mind that the list could be near endless so we will be focusing on but a few things only.

1. Each course taught by the department
2. Each lecturer within the department
3. students enrolled within a course taught by the department
4. adding and removing the above

That's the barebones of what our system will be representing. Each of these points will have their own requirements too. This will be a console based program that we create but the functionality of the program will be usable within a graphical system too. The only changes required would be how information is displayed and how data is input. This isn't really relevant to us but it's nice to know that console applications with a purpose such as this can be expanded into the graphical universe. It makes the project feel all the more purposeful!

Let's create our package directory first. I'll be calling mine *DoC*, for *Department of Computing* because calling it *CD* for *Computing Department* doesn't sound as cool plus typing "cd cd" in Windows' console would be weird. Feel free to name your package whatever you like, using the same naming conventions as a variable, as long as you remember to change my package name to your package name when writing your code! That's the easy bit done. Now, what classes do we want? Well, sticking with our university scenario outlined above, the university will have multiple departments which means our computing department is one of them, so we're going to want a class to represent that. I'll be naming this class

DoC.java for simplicity. We could also create a parent class to represent all departments within the university but I won't be doing that here. Don't worry, I'll give a list of the classes once we've walked through what we need. We will want a class to represent the courses within our department too. Each of which is taught by a lecturer. We also have students and there will definitely be some common ground between a student and a lecturer, they're both people. So we can create a *Person* class for this common ground and a *Student* and *Lecturer* class that'll inherit from *Person*.

What we have now is a list of classes that we're going to need, shown below in hierarchical order:

- DoC
- Person
    - Student
    - Lecturer (I decided not to add this class to keep the project size reasonable)
- Course

That's the only classes we will need for this project. We could add another class in a real-world project to handle communication between a database that stores all of our data but our information will be stored solely within the confines of our running program in this example. This is because "databases" isn't really introductory topic so it won't be covered in this book. Instead, our data handling and storage will take place within our DoC class.

Ok, so go ahead and create each of the .java files that we need and then open up *Person.java*, we'll start there.

We're going to need the following data in our *Person* class:

- Variables: String forename, String surname, int ID, int age, String DOBStr
- methods: getters and setters for all but ID, empty and parameterized constructors
- "package DoC;" as the first line

With that in mind, our *Person* class should look something not too far from this:

```java
package DoC;

class Person {

    protected String forename, surname, DOBStr;
    protected int id;
    public static final int UNKNOWN = -1, STUDENT = 0,
                                             LECTURER = 1;

    protected int type;

    public Person(int id) {
        this.forename = "Not Set";
        this.surname = "Not Set";
        this.DOBStr = "Not Set";
        this.id = id;
        type = Person.UNKNOWN;

    }

    public Person(String forename, String surname,
                    String DOBStr, int id, int type) {
        this.forename = forename;
        this.surname = surname;
        this.DOBStr = DOBStr;
        this.id = id;
        this.type = type;
    }

    public String getForename() {
        return forename;
    }

    public String getSurname() {
        return surname;
    }

    public String getDOBStr() {
        return DOBStr;
    }
```

```java
    public int getType() {
        return type;
    }

    public int getID() {
        return id;
    }

    public void setForename(String forename) {
        this.forename = forename;
    }

    public void setSurname(String surname) {
        this.surname = surname;
    }

    public void setDOBStr(String DOBStr) {
        this.DOBStr = DOBStr;
    }

    public void setType(int type) {
        this.type = type;
    }
}
```

Next, we'll want our *Student* class so go ahead and save *Person.java* and open up *Student.java*.

Our students will have a course of study, an average and projected grade, an attendance percentage and a current year of study. Again, we'll require getters, setters and constructors here. Don't forget, though, our *Student* will be inheriting from *Person*.

- Variables: String avgGradeStr, String projectedGradeStr, int avgGradeInt, int projectedGradeInt, double attendance, int yearOfStudy

```java
package DoC;

class Student extends Person {

    private String avgGradeStr, projectedGradeStr,
                                               course;
    private int avgGradeInt, projectedGradeInt,
                                         yearOfStudy;
    private double attendance;

    public Student (int id) {
        super(id);
        this.avgGradeStr = "0";
        this.avgGradeInt = 0;
        this.projectedGradeStr = "0";
        this.projectedGradeInt = 0;
        this.yearOfStudy = 0;
        this.attendance = 0;
        this.course = "0";
    }

    public Student(String forename, String surname,
    String DOBStr, int id, int type, String course) {

        super(forename, surname, DOBStr, id, type);
        this.avgGradeStr = "Not Set";
        this.avgGradeInt = 0;
        this.projectedGradeStr = "Not Set";
        this.projectedGradeInt = 0;
        this.yearOfStudy = 1;
        this.attendance = 100.0;
        this.course = course;
    }

    public String getAvgGradeStr() {
        return avgGradeStr;
    }

    public String getProjectedGradeStr() {
        return projectedGradeStr;
    }

    public int getAvgGradeInt() {
```

```java
        return avgGradeInt;
    }

    public int getProjectedGradeInt() {
        return projectedGradeInt;
    }

    public int getYearOfStudy() {
        return yearOfStudy;
    }

    public double getAttendace() {
        return attendance;
    }

    public String getCourse() {
        return course;
    }

    public void setAvgGradeStr(String avgGradeStr) {
        this.avgGradeStr = avgGradeStr;
    }

    public void setProjectedGradeStr(String
                                projecteGradeStr) {
        this.projectedGradeStr = projectedGradeStr;
    }

    public void setAvgGradeInt(int avgGradeInt) {
        this.avgGradeInt = avgGradeInt;
    }

    public void setProjectedGradeInt(int
                                projectGradeInt) {
        this.projectedGradeInt = projectedGradeInt;
    }

    public void setYearOfStudy(int yearOfStudy) {
        this.yearOfStudy = yearOfStudy;
    }

    public void setAttendace(double attendance) {
        this.attendance = attendance;
```

```
        }

    public void setCourse(String course) {
        this.course = course;
    }
}
```

Notice that the *Student* class has a lot to it, this is because there is a lot of data to keep track of relating to students. After all, they are taking a journey through several years of education!

We're going to tackle the *Course* class now so go ahead and open up *Course.java*.

- Variables: title, id, duration, passRate

```java
package DoC;
import java.util.*;
class Course {


    private int id, duration;
    private double passRate;

    private String title;

    public Course(int id, String title, int duration,
                                    double passRate) {
        this.id = id;
        this.title = title;
        this.duration = duration;
        this.passRate = passRate;
    }

    public String getTitle() {
        return title;
    }

    public int getId() {
        return id;
    }

    public double getPassRate() {
        return passRate;
    }

    public int getDuration() {
        return duration;
    }

    public void setTitle(String title) {
        this.title = title;
    }

    public void setPassRate(double passRate) {
        this.passRate = passRate;
    }

    public void setDuration(int duration) {
```

```
        this.duration = duration;
    }
}
```

The only class left to create is the main entry point of our program, *DoC.java*. This class will be pretty big because it brings together all the others. It needs the following:

- variables: int globalId, int temp, ArrayList<Course> courses, ArrayList<Student> students, Scanner in
- methods:
    - doStuff() - ask the user what they want to do, will be recalled regularly
    - listAllCourses()
    - listAllStudents()
    - addCourse()
    - removeCourse()
    - getCourse()
    - addStudent()
    - removeStudent()
    - getStudent()
    - viewCourse()
    - viewStudent()
    - p() - a shorthand method for printing out text

With that in mind, open up *DoC.java* and get typing! Your finished class should look like this:

```java
package DoC;
import java.util.*;

class DoC {

    int globalId=1;

    int temp = 0;

    private ArrayList<Course> courses = new
                                ArrayList<Course>();
    private ArrayList<Student> students = new
                                ArrayList<Student>();

    Scanner in = new Scanner(System.in);

    public static void main(String[] args) {
        DoC d = new DoC();

        d.doStuff();

    }

    public void doStuff() {
        int choice = 0;
        p("\n");
        p("1. Add Course");
        p("2. View Course");
        p("3. Delete Course");
        p("4. Add Student");
        p("5. View Student");
        p("6. Delete Student");
        p("7. Exit");

        try {
            choice = Integer.parseInt( in.nextLine()
                                        );
        } catch(NumberFormatException e) {
            p("You must enter a number from the
                                available options");
            doStuff();
        }
```

```java
        switch(choice) {

            case 1: //add a course
                p("Enter a course title");
                String title = in.nextLine();
                p("Enter a course duration");
                int duration = 0;
                try {
                    duration =
                Integer.parseInt(in.nextLine());
                } catch(NumberFormatException e) {
                    p("You must enter a whole
                    number for course duration.
                    Please start again");
                    doStuff();
                }

                double passRate = 0.0;

                p("Enter the course Pass Rate");
                try {
                    passRate =
Double.parseDouble(in.nextLine());
                } catch(NumberFormatException e) {
                    p("You must enter a numeric
                        value for course
                pass rate. Please start again");
                    doStuff();
                }

                addCourse(new Course(globalId++,
                title, duration, passRate) );
                p("Course has been added");
                doStuff();
            break;

            case 2: //view a course
                listAllCourses();
                if(!courses.isEmpty()) {
                    try {
```

```java
                                        temp =
        Integer.parseInt(in.nextLine());
                                }
catch(NumberFormatException e) {
                                        p("You must enter a
                number from the courses listed");
                                        doStuff();
                                }
                        }
                        else {
                                doStuff();
                        }

                        Course c = getCourse(temp);

                        if(c != null) {
                                viewCourse(c);
                        }
                        doStuff();
                break;

                case 3: //delete a course
                        listAllCourses();
                        if(!courses.isEmpty()) {
                                try {
                                        temp =
        Integer.parseInt(in.nextLine());
                                }
catch(NumberFormatException e) {
                                        p("You must enter a
                number from the courses listed");
                                        doStuff();
                                }
                        }
                        else {
                                doStuff();
                        }

                        removeCourse(temp);
                        doStuff();
                break;
```

```java
            case 4: //add Student
                    p("Enter Student Forename");
                    String forename = in.nextLine();

                    p("Enter Student Surname");
                    String surname = in.nextLine();

                    p("Enter Student DOB
                                        (dd/mm/yyyy)");
                    String dob = in.nextLine();

                    p("Enter Student course title");
                    String course = in.nextLine();

                    addStudent(new Student(forename,
                            surname, dob, globalId++,
                            Person.STUDENT, course));
                    doStuff();
                break;

            case 5: //view student
                    listAllStudents();
                    if(!students.isEmpty()) {
                        try {
                            temp =

    Integer.parseInt(in.nextLine());
                        }
catch(NumberFormatException e) {
                            p("You must enter a
                    number from the students listed");
                            doStuff();
                        }
                    }
                    else {
                        doStuff();
                    }

                    Student s = getStudent(temp);

                    if(s != null) {
                        viewStudent(s);
```

```java
                }
                doStuff();
        break;

        case 6: //delete student
                listAllStudents();
                if(!students.isEmpty()) {
                        try {
                                temp =

    Integer.parseInt(in.nextLine());
                        }
catch(NumberFormatException e) {
                                p("You must enter a
                number from the students listed");
                                doStuff();
                        }
                }
                else {
                        doStuff();
                }

                removeStudent(temp);
                doStuff();
        break;

        case 7: //exit
                System.exit(0);
        break;

        default:
                p("You must enter a number from
                        the available options");
                doStuff();
        break;
        }
    }

    public void listAllCourses() {
        if(courses.isEmpty()) {
                p("There are no courses recorded");
        }
        else {
```

```java
            for(Course c : courses) {
                p("[ID: " + c.getId() + "] " +
                                    c.getTitle() );
            }
        }
    }

    public void addCourse(Course c) {
        courses.add(c);
    }

    public void removeCourse(int id) {
        boolean removal = false;
        for(Course c : courses) {
            if(c.getId() == id) {
                p("Course: " + c.getTitle() + "
                        has been removed");
                courses.remove(c);
                removal = true;
                break;
            }
        }
        if(!removal) {
            p("No course was found with the given
                                    ID");
        }
    }

    public Course getCourse(int id) {
        for(Course c : courses) {
            if(c.getId() == id) {
                return c;
            }
        }

        return null;
    }

    public void addStudent(Student s) {
        students.add(s);
    }

    public void removeStudent(int id) {
```

```java
            boolean removal = false;
            for(Student s : students) {
                if(s.getId() == id) {
                    p("Student: " + s.getForename() +
                        " " + s.getSurname() +
                        " has been removed");
                    students.remove(s);
                    removal = true;

                    break;
                }
            }

            if(!removal) {
                p("No student was found with the given
                                                    ID");
            }
    }

    public Student getStudent(int id) {
        for(Student s : students) {
            if(s.getId() == id) {
                return s;
            }
        }

        return null;
    }

    public void listAllStudents() {
        if(students.isEmpty()) {
            p("There are no students recorded");
        }
        else {
            for(Student s : students) {
                p("[ID: " + s.getId() + "] " +
                        s.getForename() +
                    " " + s.getSurname() );
            }
        }
    }

    public void viewCourse(Course c) {
```

```java
        p(c.getTitle());
        p("Duration: " + c.getDuration() + "
                                    Year(s)");
        p("Pass Rate: " + c.getPassRate() + "%");

    }

    public void viewStudent(Student s) {
        p(s.getForename() + " " + s.getSurname());
        p(s.getDOBStr());
        p(s.getCourse());
    }
    static void p(String m) {
        System.out.println(m);
    }
}
```

Well, that's it. If you get all this code written up and compiled, you will end up with a functional program that allows you to create courses and students as well as viewing and deleting the records you create. It's a pretty simple program in terms of functionality and intends to show a working example of all aspects of programming with Java that I have covered in this book. I almost forgot, to compile a package you must be outside of the package directory. The screenshot below illustrates this:

Here, I am currently in the Java directory which contains the DoC directory. I use "javac DoC/DoC.java" to compile DoC.java which also compiles all other Java files that are required. Alternatively, I could have typed "javac DoC/*.java" to compile all Java files within the DoC package.

Here's a couple of screenshots of the program in action so you know what to expect:

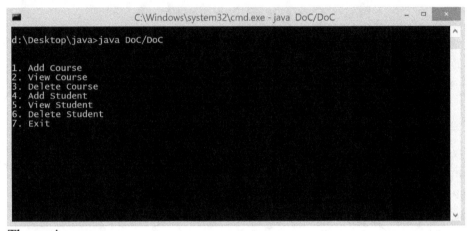

The main menu

```
C:\Windows\system32\cmd.exe - java DoC/DoC

5. View Student
6. Delete Student
7. Exit
1
Enter a course title
Computer Science
Enter a course duration
3
Enter the course Pass Rate
100
Course has been added


1. Add Course
2. View Course
3. Delete Course
4. Add Student
5. View Student
6. Delete Student
7. Exit
```

Option 1 with input (adding a course)

```
C:\Windows\system32\cmd.exe - java DoC/DoC

3. Delete Course
4. Add Student
5. View Student
6. Delete Student
7. Exit
2
[ID: 1] Computer Science
1
Computer Science
Duration: 3 Year(s)
Pass Rate: 100.0%


1. Add Course
2. View Course
3. Delete Course
4. Add Student
5. View Student
6. Delete Student
7. Exit
```

Option 2 followed by ID 1 (Viewing a course)

173

```
2. View Course
3. Delete Course
4. Add Student
5. View Student
6. Delete Student
7. Exit
3
[ID: 1] Computer Science
1
Course: Computer Science has been removed


1. Add Course
2. View Course
3. Delete Course
4. Add Student
5. View Student
6. Delete Student
7. Exit
2
There are no courses recorded
```

Option 3 followed by ID 1 and then Option 2 (Deleting a course)

```
6. Delete Student
7. Exit
4
Enter Student Forename
Tim
Enter Student Surname
Talbot
Enter Student DOB (dd/mm/yyyy)
01/01/1970
Enter Student course title
CS


1. Add Course
2. View Course
3. Delete Course
4. Add Student
5. View Student
6. Delete Student
7. Exit
```

Option 4 with input (Adding a student)

```
C:\Windows\system32\cmd.exe - java  DoC/DoC

3. Delete Course
4. Add Student
5. View Student
6. Delete Student
7. Exit
5
[ID: 2] Tim Talbot
2
Tim Talbot
01/01/1970
CS

1. Add Course
2. View Course
3. Delete Course
4. Add Student
5. View Student
6. Delete Student
7. Exit
```

Option 5 followed by ID 2 (Viewing a student)

```
C:\Windows\system32\cmd.exe - java  DoC/DoC

1. Add Course
2. View Course
3. Delete Course
4. Add Student
5. View Student
6. Delete Student
7. Exit
6
[ID: 2] Tim Talbot
2
Student: Tim Talbot has been removed

1. Add Course
2. View Course
3. Delete Course
4. Add Student
5. View Student
6. Delete Student
7. Exit
```

Option 6 followed by ID 2 (Deleting a student)

```
■                              C:\Windows\system32\cmd.exe              _  □  ×
3. Delete Course                                                              ^
4. Add Student
5. View Student
6. Delete Student
7. Exit
6
[ID: 2] Tim Talbot
2
Student: Tim Talbot has been removed

1. Add Course
2. View Course
3. Delete Course
4. Add Student
5. View Student
6. Delete Student
7. Exit
7
d:\Desktop\java>_                                                            ∨
```

Option 7 (Exiting the program)

As I mentioned previous, our program is pretty simple in terms of what
it does. It could be almost infinitely expanded and nurtured into a full
scale representation of a university system but I just wanted to stick to
essential functionality for the purposes of putting all the stuff we've
looked at into practice. Now, let's look at the classes! *Person, Student* and
Course are all really self-explanatory and you should be able to
understand these classes quite well if you've followed through the book
or are familiar with Java so that's all I will say about them. the *DoC* class
is a little more in-depth and, although it only uses the stuff we've
learned, will get a more thorough explanation.

First off, we have the start of our class and variable introductions.

```java
package DoC;
import java.util.*;

class DoC {

        int globalId=1;

        int temp = 0;

        private ArrayList<Course> courses = new
                                    ArrayList<Course>();
        private ArrayList<Student> students = new
                                    ArrayList<Student>();
```

176

```
Scanner in = new Scanner(System.in);
```

In order of appearance, we are declaring which package our class is a part of, importing the java.util.*; package so we can use the *Scanner* class and then opening our class. Following this, we have five (5) variable declarations; two *ints*, two *ArrayLists* and a *Scanner*. The first integer variable is used to provide each course and student that we create with a unique ID and it is incremented each time it is used. We could have created another separate integer variable here so we would have a unique ID for both course and student with independence of each other but for our purpose, this will suffice. The second integer we have, *temp*, is simply used to store input from the user so we can act upon it. Following this, we have two *ArrayLists* which serve to store our *Course* and *Student* objects. Finally, we declare and instantiate a *Scanner* object so we can get our input from the user when we ask for it. Next up we have our *main()* method, which is nice and simple in this case. We create an instantiation of the *DoC* class and then call the *doStuff()* method via this newly instantiated object. This is how you avoid having to declare all your variables and methods as static!

```
public static void main(String[] args) {
    DoC d = new DoC();
    d.doStuff();
}
```

Following *main()* is the *doStuff()* method which is essentially the core of this program. It asks the user what they want to do, listens for input and then runs a *switch* block to act upon this input. If the user doesn't input an appropriate option, they are informed. This includes both options outside the range of the switch and non-numeric input. No matter what course of action is taken within the *doStuff()* method, it will call itself again (with the exception of the user requesting to exit the program).

```
public void doStuff() {
    int choice = 0;
    p("\n");
```

177

```
p("1. Add Course");
p("2. View Course");
p("3. Delete Course");
p("4. Add Student");
p("5. View Student");
p("6. Delete Student");
p("7. Exit");

try {
    choice = Integer.parseInt( in.nextLine()
                                             );
} catch(NumberFormatException e) {
    p("You must enter a number from the
                available options");
    doStuff();
}

switch(choice) {
```

This is the first part of *doStuff()* in which you can see that we declare and initialise an integer variable to zero. This is to store the user's input and be used as the flag in our *switch* block a bit further down. We print a new line incorrectly, you should use Java's *System.getProperty()* method to get the new line character but I have just used \n instead because this works fine on Windows. Following this is a print out of 7 options. We then await the user input and attempt to convert it to an integer and assign it to our *choice* variable. This takes place within a *try-catch* block, of course.

The *switch* has 7 cases and the *default* case. Each of the 7 cases, of course, correspond to the 7 options given to the user which are shown in the above code snippet.

```
case 1: //add a course
    p("Enter a course title");
    String title = in.nextLine();
    p("Enter a course duration");
    int duration = 0;
    try {
        duration = Integer.parseInt(in.nextLine());
    } catch(NumberFormatException e) {
```

```
                p("You must enter a whole number for course
                        duration. Please start again");
            doStuff();
        }

        double passRate = 0.0;

        p("Enter the course Pass Rate");
        try {
            passRate = Double.parseDouble(in.nextLine());
        } catch(NumberFormatException e) {
            p("You must enter a numeric value for course
                    pass rate. Please start again");
            doStuff();
        }

        addCourse(new Course(globalId++, title, duration,
                                        passRate) );
        p("Course has been added");
        doStuff();
break;
```

This is the first case in our *switch*, for adding a course. First, we ask the user to input a course title and then create a *String* to store this title with a value provided by *in.nextLine()*. Then we ask the user for the course duration, this is converted to an *integer* within a *try-catch* block to ensure any *NumberFormatException* exceptions are taken care of. If they do arise, *doStuff()* is called again to restart the process, along with informing the user why. Finally, we ask the user to input the course pass rate as a *double* which is again converted to the correct format of *double* within a *try-catch* block. If all goes well, the *addCourse()* method is called and passed a new *Course* object before finally informing the user that the course has indeed been added and then calling *doStuff()* again. Case 4, to add a new student, follows the same pattern of asking the user for input and then taking that input to create a new object and passing it to the *addStudent()* method. Thus, case 4 will not require any further explanation.

Case 2 allows the viewing of courses. This is also similar to case 5 which allows the viewing of students so this explanation will also apply in both cases.

```
case 2: //view a course
      listAllCourses();
      if(!courses.isEmpty()) {
            try {
                  temp = Integer.parseInt(in.nextLine());
            } catch(NumberFormatException e) {
                  p("You must enter a number from the
                                      courses listed");
                  doStuff();
            }
      }
      else {
            doStuff();
      }
      Course c = getCourse(temp);
      if(c != null) {
            viewCourse(c);
      }
      doStuff();
break;
```

The first thing we do is call a method called *listAllCourses()* (or *listAllStudents()* for case 5) which prints out the name of every course object stored within the *courses* ArrayList. If there are no courses, that fact will be displayed instead. Then we have an *if-else* block which says if the *courses* ArrayList is **not** empty, ask the user which course they want to view and await their input which is converted to an *integer* within a *try-catch* block. If the *courses* list is empty, we will simply recall the *doStuff()* method. Following this *if-else,* we attempt to get the *Course* object based on the user-inputted ID, via the *getCourse()* method. If this **does not** return *null* we then call the *viewCourse()* method with the *course* object as a parameter. In any circumstance, the *doStuff()* method is again called at the end of the case. Don't forget, the same functionality occurs in case 5, the only difference being that case 5 refers to viewing students instead of courses.

Case 3 is for deleting courses and again resembles another case in regards to students, case 6. Case 3 calls *listAllCourses()*, takes a user input and then attempts to remove the given input from the *courses* ArrayList via the *deleteCourse()* method, which takes an *integer* ID as an argument. Again, *doStuff()* is called before the case finishes. Finally, case 7 simply says "System.exit(0);" in order to exit the program gracefully.

Let's take a look at the other methods within our program, then.

We have *listAllCourses()* and *listAllStudents()* which both behave the same way except one refers to the *courses* ArrayList and the other the *students* ArrayList. These methods use an *if-else* to check whether the respective ArrayList is empty and if so it tells the user, if not then it'll use a *for* loop to cycle through each element of the ArrayList and display the name of the course or student.

```
public void listAllCourses() {
    if(courses.isEmpty()) {
        p("There are no courses recorded");
    }
    else {
        for(Course c : courses) {
            p("[ID: " + c.getId() + "] " +
                            c.getTitle() );
        }
    }
}
```

```
public void listAllStudents() {
    if(students.isEmpty()) {
        p("There are no students recorded");
    }
    else {
        for(Student s : students) {
            p("[ID: " + s.getId() + "] " +
                s.getForename() +
                " " + s.getSurname() );
        }
    }
}
```

Then there's *addCourse()* and *addStudent()* which are one line methods that use the *ArrayLists add()* method to add an object to the list. These methods could be extended to ensure that we're not adding a duplicate or something like that but for our purpose, this is fine.

removeCourse() and *removeStudent()* take an *integer* ID that corresponds to a *course* or *student* object (the ID stored within the object, not the index of the object within the ArrayList) and then searches through the respective list via a *for* loop, checking the IDs for a match. If a match is found, a local *boolean* is set to true so we know that there has been a deletion, the user is informed and finally the object is removed from the list before the *for* loop is exited with the *break* keyword. If there is no deletion, the *boolean* remains *false* and an *if* block is executed to inform the user that no match was found with the given ID.

```java
public void removeCourse(int id) {
    boolean removal = false;
    for(Course c : courses) {
        if(c.getId() == id) {
            p("Course: " + c.getTitle() + " has been
                                            removed");
            courses.remove(c);
            removal = true;
            break;
        }
    }
    if(!removal) {
        p("No course was found with the given ID");
    }
}


public void removeStudent(int id) {
    boolean removal = false;
    for(Student s : students) {
        if(s.getId() == id) {
            p("Student: " + s.getForename() + " " +
                            s.getSurname() +
                " has been removed");
```

```
            students.remove(s);
            removal = true;
            break;
        }
    }

    if(!removal) {
        p("No student was found with the given ID");
    }
}
```

We then have *getCourse()* and *getStudent()* which work in a very similar way to *removeCourse()* and *removeStudent()* in the sense that the methods both take an *integer* parameter and use it to identify an object within a list via a *for* loop. The difference being that *getCourse()* and *getStudent()* return the respective object if found and *null* otherwise.

All that's left to look at now is *viewCourse()* and *viewStudent()* which both do what they say they do and that's view a course or a student! These methods just take a *course* or *student* object and then access the data within that object in order to display it to the user. Quite simple really.

```
public void viewCourse(Course c) {
    p(c.getTitle());
    p("Duration: " + c.getDuration() + "
                                    Year(s)");
    p("Pass Rate: " + c.getPassRate() + "%");

}

public void viewStudent(Student s) {
    p(s.getForename() + " " + s.getSurname());
    p(s.getDOBStr());
    p(s.getCourse());
}
```

You may have also noticed that anywhere there is output, I use the method *p()*. Granted, this could have been named more appropriately but *p* represents *print* and so it seemed to fit. This method takes a *String* and then prints it out using *System.out.println();* and I have done this for two reasons. One is to save me having to type *System.out.println();* every time I wanted to output something to the user and the other is, if this was a real world project with the possibility of being used somewhere else where the method of displaying data to the user was unknown, only the body of the *p()* method would have to be changed to do this.

Chapter 17: Where to go from here

Well, now you've made it to the final chapter which means you've studied the foundations of the Java programming language and should be able to go away and write your very own programs. But all we've done is look at the basics, what's next?

That's a question best answered once you have decided what it is you want to be doing with your new found knowledge. If you're just looking for a job as a Java programmer, I'd recommend looking at learning about multithreading and then you'll probably be ready. Experience is valued over knowledge in the industry but if you can show you know the language, that's all that really matters.

App Development

Java is used for developing applications on the Android OS; mobile app development. If this is a path you want to take, you'll need to look at the Android development tutorials provided by Google. There is some XML involved with app development but the functionality of apps will be written in Java, of course.

Storing Data

A lot of programs, apps or otherwise, require the storage of data. There's several ways you can go about storing data. Firstly, you could go forth and study reading and writing to files with Java. I originally planned to have a chapter on this but I decided against it because I felt it was a bit more than required for an introduction to Java. Then there's property files, this is essentially reading and writing to a file with the specific intention of storing properties only in key-value format. Finally, there are databases. Java can communicate with MySQL, PostGreSQL, SQLite and other SQL servers with the aid of a Java database Connector Driver (JDBC). A JDBC is an external jar that you import into your projects in order to communicate with SQL servers, I am only familiar with the JDBC drivers for MySQL and PostGreSQL. This is a rather advanced topic but it is your alternative to storing data. Android apps use SQLite for local database storage, if needed.

Graphical User Interface

Perhaps you want to create graphical Java programs. Java provides an API called SWING which provides you with the ability to create a Graphical User Interface. You can learn more about this via the Java online documentation.

JavaFX is a newer API that is slowly replacing SWING so it is best to start there if you're new to the Java GUI scene.

JavaServer Pages (JSP)

Java provides *JavaServer Pages,* known as JSP. JSP is a server side programming language for web development. It is similar to PHP and ASP in that respect, the difference being that it uses Java. A web server that supports JSP by means of a servlet container such as Apache Tomcat is required in order to run JSP code. I wouldn't recommend learning Java for the sole purpose of web development, there are other technologies much more suited to the task.

Applets

Applets are Java Applications that are delivered to the user via a web page. These applications still run on the users' local JVM so they are still required to have a JVM installed and must acquire permission from the user in order to run.

Network Programming

Understanding network programming with Java is definitely a useful skill to add to your arsenal of programming knowledge. I'd definitely recommend researching multithreading before network programming, though. Network programming means communicating across the internet via your code. So you'd make a server and a client and have them communicate, for example.

Timing Code Execution

You may recall that in the chapter on recursion, I said that we'd take a look at timing the execution of our code to see which is quicker. So let's get to it! In that chapter, we wrote a method for calculating the *n*th Fibonacci number using recursion and I stated that, although a good demonstration of recursion, it's not a very computationally efficient technique for the problem at hand and it would in fact be better to simply add up all the numbers between 0 and **n** instead to find **n**. So here's that original *Fib* class with an additional method which does just that:

```java
class Fib {

    static long startTime   = 0;
    static long endTime     = 0;
    static long duration    = 0;
    static long duration2   = 0;

    public static void main(String[] args) {
        System.out.println("Recursive: ");

        startTime = System.nanoTime();
        for(int i=1; i <= 30; i++)
            System.out.println(fibN(i));

        endTime = System.nanoTime();
        duration = (endTime - startTime);

        System.out.println("execution took " +
                            duration + " nanoseconds");

        System.out.println("Non-Recursive: ");

        startTime = System.nanoTime();
        for(int i=1; i <= 30; i++)
            System.out.println(fibN2(i));

        endTime = System.nanoTime();
        duration2 = (endTime - startTime);
```

```java
        System.out.println("execution took " +
                        duration2 + " nanoseconds");

        System.out.println(duration + " vs \n" +
                                        duration2);
    }

    static int fibN(int n) {
        if(n <= 1) {
            return n;
        }
        else {
            return fibN(n-1) + fibN(n-2);
        }
    }

    static int fibN2(int n) {
        int current        = 1;
        int previous       = 0;
        int next     = 1;
        int temp     = 0;

        for(int i = 1; i < n; i++ ) {

            temp = current;
            next = previous+current;
            current = next;
            previous = temp;
        }

        return next;
    }
}
```

I won't explain the additional method because it's simple enough, we start at the beginning of the Fibonacci sequence and add all numbers up to **n**. What's important here is the use of *long* and *System.nanoTime();*. *System.nanoTime()* returns the current time in nanoseconds. What we do is store this value in a *long* before we begin our method execution, a loop which calls a method, in this case, and then get a new value from *System.nanoTime()* after the loop finishes. We then subtract the new nanotime from the starting nanotime to get our duration of execution in nanoseconds. Some folk argue that *System.getCurrentMillis()* is more or less accurate but many things affect accuracy including the machine on which the JVM is running, for example. Anyway, this is the general logic behind timing code execution. If you want to have consistent results when comparing the timing of different techniques, it's best to use the same machine for all timing. Don't use a laptop to time *FibN()* and then a extremely high performance pc to time *FibN2()*. Try this class to get a feel for timing code execution.

A Final Word

I'd like to say thank you to you for purchasing this book and I hope you have found it as useful as I intended it to be. If not, or even if so, I'd love to know why. Feel free to drop me some feedback at:

aitpwjb@timtalbot.co.uk

This is indeed my first publication and so I would love to know how I've done, good or bad. So I can ensure any future authoring is improved for you guys.

Also, I've read through this book several times and while every effort has been made to ensure that there are no typos, errors in code or any other problems, I am only human. If you do happen to discover any such occurrence, please drop me an email and I'll update my site to reflect this.

Finally, if you get stuck with anything, drop me an email. Please bear in mind that I get a lot of emails so I can't reply to them all at once. There may even come a time when I can't possibly reply to them all, but I will do my best to get back to you if I at all can!

Thank you,

Tim Talbot.

Appendix A

So, all those exercises you done... here's the solutions for them!

Chapter 1

Exercise 1

```java
//import class needed to read from console
import java.util.Scanner;

class HelloWorldIsBoring
{
    //declare variable to read from console
    static Scanner in = new Scanner(System.in);

    public static void main(String[] args)
    {
        //ask user what to do
        System.out.println("What shall I do for
                                        you?");
        System.out.println("1)Repeat your
                    name\n2)Repeat your
                    age\n3)Run away and hide
                    (exit program)");

        //variable declaration and assignment
        int response=0;

        //(advanced) error catching
        try
        {
            //get user response
            response =
                Integer.parseInt(in.nextLine());
        }
        catch(NumberFormatException nfe)
        //if response is not a number...
        {
            //tell user of error and die
            System.out.println("You did not enter a
                    number. Exiting program");
```

```java
            //System.out.println(nfe.toString());

            System.exit(0);
        }

        //declare string variable
        String temp=""; //store response

        //flow control switch statement
        switch(response)
        {
            case 1:
                System.out.print("What is your
                                        name? ");
                temp = in.nextLine();
                System.out.println("Hello, " +
                                        temp);
            break;

            case 2:

                System.out.println("How old are
                                        you?");
                temp = in.nextLine();
                System.out.println("You are " +
                            temp + " years old!");
            break;

            case 3:
                System.out.println("Exiting
                                        program!");
                System.exit(0);
            break;

            default:
                System.out.println("Unknown
                        Command. Exiting Program!");
                System.exit(0);
            break;
        }//end switch
    }//end main()
}//end class
```

- creates a new line character, at least on windows.
- Java uses System.getProperty("line.separator"); for a platform-independent line separator

Exercise 3

```java
//import class needed to read from console
import java.util.Scanner;

class HelloWorldIsBoring
{
    //declare variable to read from console
    static Scanner new_in = new Scanner(System.in);

    public static void main(String[] args)
    {
        //ask user what to do
        System.out.println("What shall I do for
                                            you?");
        System.out.println("1)Repeat your name\n
                        2)Repeat your age\n
                        3)Run away and hide (exit
                                        program)");

        //variable declaration and assignment
        int response=0;

        //(advanced) error catching
        try
        {
            //get user response
            response =
            Integer.parseInt(new_in.nextLine());
        }
        catch(NumberFormatException nfe)
        //if response is not a number...
        {
            //tell user of error and die
            System.out.println("You did not enter a
                        number. Exiting program");
            //System.out.println(nfe.toString());
```

```java
                System.exit(0);
        }

        //declare string variable
        String temp=""; //store response

        //flow control switch statement
        switch(response)
        {
            case 1:
                System.out.print("What is your
                                        name? ");
                temp = new_in.nextLine();
                System.out.println("Hello, " +
                                        temp);
            break;

            case 2:

                System.out.println("How old are
                                        you?");
                temp = new_in.nextLine();
                System.out.println("You are " +
                                        temp + " years
                                        old!");
            break;

            case 3:
                System.out.println("Exiting
                                        program!");
                System.exit(0);
            break;

            default:
                System.out.println("Unknown
                        Command. Exiting Program!");
                System.exit(0);
            break;
        }//end switch
    }//end main()
}//end class
```

```
public static void main(String[] args)
or
public static void main(String... args)
```

Chapter 6

Exercise 1

```
for(int i=1; i<=10; i++) {
    int n = (i* (i+1) ) / 2;
    System.out.println(n);
}
```

Exercise 2

```
int count = 1;

while(count<=10) {
    int n = (count * (count+1) ) / 2;
    count++;
}
```

Exercise 3a

```
int i =1;
for(; i<=10; i++) {
    int n = (i* (i+1) ) / 2;
    System.out.println(n);
}
```

Exercise 3b

```
for(int i = 1; ; i++) {
    int n = (i* (i+1) ) / 2;
    System.out.println(n);

    if(i==10) {
        break;
    }
}
```

Exercise 3c

```
for(int i = 1; i<=10; ) {
    int n = (i* (i+1) ) / 2;
    System.out.println(n);
    i++;
}
```

Exercise 3d

```
for(int i=1; ;) {
    int n = (i* (i+1) ) / 2;
    System.out.println(n);

    if(i==10) break;
    i++;
}
```

Exercise 3e

```
int i = 1;
for(; i<=10; ) {
    int n = (i* (i+1) ) / 2;
    System.out.println(n);
    i++;
}
```

Exercise 3f

```
int i=1;

for(;; i++) {
    int n = (i* (i+1) ) / 2;
    System.out.println(n);

    if(i==10) break;
}
```

Exercise 3g

```java
int i=1;

for(;;) {
    int n = (i* (i+1) ) / 2;
    System.out.println(n);

    if(i==10) break;

    i++;
}
```

Exercise 4

```java
int[] arr = new int[10];

for(int i=0; i<arr.length; i++) {
    arr[i] = i+1;
}

for(int n : arr) {
    System.out.println(n);
}
```

```
//while loop
int count = 0;
while(count <= 10) {
    if(count % 2 != 0) {
        System.out.println(count);
    }
    count++;
}

//do-while
//even if count is above 10, this loop
//will print the value once as long as it
//is not even, so we change the 'if' to
//ensure this does't happen thus making this
//a bad choice for this particular task
int count = 0;
do {
    if(count % 2 != 0 && count <= 10) {
        System.out.println(count);
    }
    count++;
} while(count <= 10);

//for
for(int i = 0; i <= 10; i++) {
    if(i % 2 != 0) {
        System.out.println(i);
    }
}
```

Chapter 12

```java
class main {

    public static void main(String[] args) {

        Temperature t = new Temperature(30d,
Temperature.CELSIUS);

        System.out.println("celsius: " +
t.getCelsius());
        System.out.println("fahrenheit: " +
t.getFahrenheit());

        t.setCelsius(15d);

        System.out.println("celsius: " +
t.getCelsius());
        System.out.println("fahrenheit: " +
t.getFahrenheit());

        t.setFahrenheit(100d);

        System.out.println("celsius: " +
t.getCelsius());
        System.out.println("fahrenheit: " +
t.getFahrenheit());

    }
}
```

```java
class Temperature {

    //variables for celsius and fahrenheit
    private double c;
    private double f;

    /** flags for switch statement used to
     * identify celsius or fahrenheit
     **/
    public static final int CELSIUS        = 0;
    public static final int FAHRENHEIT  = 1;



    /**
     * Constructor.
     * double temp - temperature
     * int type - temperature units, CELS or FAHR
     **/
    public Temperature(double temp, int type) {

        switch(type) {
            case CELSIUS:
                c = temp;
                f = toFahrenheit(c);
            break;

            case FAHRENHEIT:
                f = temp;
                c = toCelsius(f);
            break;

            default:
                c = 0;
                f = 0;
        }
    } //end constructor

    private double toFahrenheit(double c) {

        double fahrenheit = (c * (9d/5d)) + 32d;

        return fahrenheit;
```

```java
    }

    double toCelsius(double f) {

        double celsius = (f - 32d) * (5d/9d);

        return celsius;
    }

    public double getCelsius() {
        return c;
    }

    public double getFahrenheit() {
        return f;
    }

    public void setCelsius(double c) {
        this.c = c;
        f = toFahrenheit(c);
    }

    public void setFahrenheit(double f) {
        this.f = f;
        c = toCelsius(f);
    }
}
```

Chapter 14

```java
import java.util.ArrayList;

class Account {

    /**
     *    These values will be used as flags
     *    to determine whether to add or remove
     *    a value from the account balance.
     *    we will access them by using dot notation
     *    in a static contact. i.e. Account.ADD or
     *    Account.SUB, outside this class.
     **/
    public static final int ADD = 0, SUB = 1;

    /**
     *    We could use several fields for
     *    title, forename and surname instead
     *    but for the sake of simplicity, we
     *    will just use a single string.
     **/

    private int accountNumber;
    private String accountHolder;

    /**
     *    Remember chapter 3 regarding currency
     *    (float/double should not be used),
     *    I'm ignoring that for the sake of simplicity.
     *    BigDecimal is better for currency due to
     *    accuracy.
     **/

    private double accountBalance;
    private double transactionFee;
    private ArrayList<Double> transactions = new
ArrayList<Double>();


    //for business and commercial accounts only
```

```java
    private String businessType;


    public Account(String accountHolder, double
        accountBalance, double transactionFee) {

        this.accountHolder = accountHolder;
        this.accountBalance = accountBalance;
        this.transactionFee = transactionFee;

        transactions.add(accountBalance);
    }

    public Account(String accountHolder, double
        accountBalance, double transactionFee,
                        String businessType) {

        this.accountHolder = accountHolder;
        this.accountBalance = accountBalance;
        this.transactionFee = transactionFee;
        this.businessType = businessType;

        transactions.add(accountBalance);
    }
    public int getAccountNumber() {
        return accountNumber;
    }

    public String getAccountHolder() {
        return accountHolder;
    }

    public double getAccountBalance() {
        return accountBalance;
    }

    public double getTransactionFee() {
        return transactionFee;
    }

    public ArrayList<Double> getTransactions() {
        return transactions;
    }
```

```java
    public String getBusinessType() {
        return businessType;
    }

    public void doTransaction(int transactionType,
                                    double value) {

        switch(transactionType) {
            case ADD:
                accountBalance += value;
                transactions.add(value);
            break;

            case SUB:
                accountBalance -= value;
                transactions.add(value*-1);
                accountBalance -= (value *
                        (transactionFee/100d) );
            break;
        }
    }

    public void setTransactionFee(double transactionFee)
    {
        this.transactionFee = transactionFee;
    }

    public void setAccountHolder(String accountHolder) {
        this.accountHolder = accountHolder;
    }

    public void setBusinessType(String businessType) {
        this.businessType = businessType;
    }
}
```

```java
class BankingSystem {

    public static void main(String[] args) {

        PersonalAccount a1 = new
PersonalAccount("Personal", 100d, 10d);
        BusinessAccount a2 = new
BusinessAccount("Business", 100d, 10d, "Government");
        CommercialAccount a3 = new
CommercialAccount("Commercial", 100d, 10d, "Medical");

        //get account holders
        p("a1 Account Holder: " +
                        a1.getAccountHolder());
        p("a2 Account Holder: " +
                        a2.getAccountHolder());
        p("a3 Account Holder: " +
                a3.getAccountHolder()+"\n");

        //get account balances
        p("a1 Balance: " + a1.getAccountBalance());
        p("a2 Balance: " + a2.getAccountBalance());
        p("a3 Balance: " +
                a3.getAccountBalance()+"\n");

        //get account transaction fees
        p("a1 Transaction Fee: " +
                        a1.getTransactionFee());
        p("a2 Transaction Fee: " +
                        a2.getTransactionFee());
        p("a3 Transaction Fee: " +
                a3.getTransactionFee()+"\n");

        //get account business typs
        p("a1 Business Type: " +
                        a1.getBusinessType());
        p("a2 Business Type: " +
                        a2.getBusinessType());
        p("a3 Business Type: " +
                a3.getBusinessType()+"\n");

        p("Adding 25 to a1");
```

```java
        a1.doTransaction(Account.ADD, 25.0d);
        p("a1 Balance: " + a1.getAccountBalance());

        p("Subtracting 10 from a2");
        a2.doTransaction(Account.SUB, 10.0d);
        p("a2 Balance: " + a2.getAccountBalance());
        p("remember that " + a2.getTransactionFee()
        +"% of withdrawals is also deducted from the
                                overall balance");

        p("\nAccount a2 Transaction History");

        for(Double d : a2.getTransactions() ) {
            String type = (d>0d) ? "Deposited" :
                                    "Withdrawn";
            p(Double.toString(d) + " " + type);
        }
    }

    //I've added this method for my own convenience
    static void p(String m) {
        System.out.println(m);
    }
}
```

BusinessAccount.java

```java
class BusinessAccount extends Account {

    public BusinessAccount(String accountHolder, double
        accountBalance, double transactionFee, String
                                        businessType) {

        super(accountHolder, accountBalance,
                    transactionFee, businessType);
    }
}
```

CommercialAccount.java

```java
class CommercialAccount extends Account {

    public CommercialAccount(String accountHolder,
    double accountBalance, double transactionFee,
                            String businessType) {

        super(accountHolder, accountBalance,
                    transactionFee, businessType);
    }
}
```

PersonalAccount.java

```java
class PersonalAccount extends Account {

    public PersonalAccount(String accountHolder, double
                accountBalance, double transactionFee) {

        super(accountHolder, accountBalance,
                                    transactionFee);
    }

    public String getBusinessType() {
        return "Personal Accounts do not have a
                                business type";
    }
}
```

www.ingramcontent.com/pod-product-compliance
Lightning Source LLC
LaVergne TN
LVHW062316060326
832902LV00013B/2244